THE

OF
EATING
OUT

ALSO BY JOSEPH CONNOLLY

Fiction

Poor Souls

This Is It

Stuff

Summer Things

Winter Breaks

It Can't Go On

S.O.S.

The Works

Love Is Strange

Jack the Lad and Bloody Mary

England's Lane

Boys and Girls

Non-fiction

Collecting Modern First Editions

P. G. Wodehouse: An Illustrated Biography

Jerome K. Jerome: A Critical Biography

Modern First Editions: Their Value to Collectors

The Penguin Book Quiz Book

Children's Modern First Editions: Their Value to Collectors

Beside the Seaside

All Shook Up: A Flash of the Fifties

Christmas and How to Survive It

Wodehouse

Faber and Faber: Eighty Years of Book Cover Design

JOSEPH CONNOLLY

THE A-Z

OF EATING OUT

 Thames & Hudson

First published in the United Kingdom
in 2014 by Thames & Hudson Ltd,
181A High Holborn, London
WC1V 7QX

The A–Z of Eating Out © 2014
Joseph Connolly

Designed by This-Side

British Library Cataloguing-in-Publication Data
A catalogue record for this book is available from
the British Library

ISBN 978-0-500-51736-9

Printed and bound in China by Toppan Leefung
Printing Limited

Picture Credits

15 From U. Dubois and E. Bernard,
*La Cuisine classique: études pratiques, raisonnées
et démonstratives de l'école français appliquée au
service à la Russe*, Paris, 1886; 24 Charles
Phelps Cushing/ClassicStock/Topfoto;
27 © Illustrated London News Ltd/Mary
Evans; 42 Photo Bert Hardy © Hulton-
Deutsch Colleaction/Corbis; 47 From
P. Mac Orlan and C. Laborde, *Rues et
visages de Londres*, Paris, 1928; 75 Chris
Ware/Hulton Archive/Getty Images;
96 Interfoto/akg-images; 125 Jacques
Rouchon/akg-images; 136 Collection
IM/Kharbine-Tapabor/Art Archive;
147 © Photo Collection Alexander Alland,
Sr/Corbis; 151 Jacques Rouchon/akg-
images; 165 Musée d'Orsay, Paris; 175 ©
Bettmann/Corbis; 193 Private Collection;
201 Mary Evans Picture Library; 227 ©
Bettmann/Corbis; 239 Museo Civico 'Ala
Ponzone', Cremona; 253 © H. Armstrong
Roberts/ClassicStock/Corbis

To find out about all our publications,
please visit **www.thamesandhudson.com**

There you can subscribe to our e-newsletter,
browse or download our current catalogue,
and buy any titles that are in print.

TO TERENCE CONRAN
THE FOUNDER OF THE MODERN FEAST

MENU

·····················

INTRODUCTION 10

ALL-YOU-CAN-EAT BUFFET 13
AMUSE-BOUCHE 13
APERITIF 16
ATMOSPHERE 19

B

BAR 21
BARGAIN LUNCH 23
BILL 25
BISTRO 28
BOOKING 29
BRASSERIE 32
BREAD AND BUTTER 34
BREAKFAST 35
BRUNCH 36
BURGERS 37
BUSINESS LUNCH 38
BUZZ 39
BYO 40

C

CAFES 43
CARVERY 44
CASINOS 45
CELEBRATIONS 46
CHAINS 46
CHAMPAGNE 49
CHARITY DINNERS 51
CHEESE 52
CHILDREN 53
CHINESE 54
CHIPS 56
CHRISTMAS 57
CLOAKROOM 58
CLUBS 58
COFFEE 61
COMFORT 62
COMPLAINING 63
CONCEPTS 66
CONDIMENTS 67
CONVERSATION 67
CORDON BLEU 69
CORPORATE ENTERTAINING 69
COURSES 70

D

DECOR 73
DESIGNATED DRIVER 76
DINNER 76
DOORMEN 77
DRINKING 78
DUMPS 79

ETIQUETTE 81
EXCUSE FINGERS 84

FAMILY MEALS 87
FASHION 87
FAST FOOD 89
FINE DINING 90
FISH 92
FOOD POISONING 93
FOOD/WINE 94
FORAGING 95
FOREIGN 97
FORMAL DINNERS 98
FRENCH 99
FRONT OF HOUSE 101
FUSION 102

GASTROPUBS 105
GLAMOUR 107
GOING DUTCH 108
GOURMETS AND GOURMANDS 110
GREASY SPOONS 111
GUESTS 112

HEALTH AND SAFETY 115
HOSTS 116
HOTELS 116

INDIAN 119
INEDIBILIA 120
INTERNATIONAL FOOD 121
INVITATIONS 122
ITALIAN 123

JACKET REQUIRED 127

KITCHEN TABLE 131

LADIES WHO LUNCH 134
LE PATRON MANGE ICI 135
LIQUID LUNCH 135
LITTLE PLATES 137
LONDON 139
LOOS 140
LUNCH 142

MENUS 145
MOTHER'S DAY 149
MUSIC 150

NAMES OF RESTAURANTS 154
NEW YEAR'S EVE 154
NOSE TO TAIL 156

OFF MENU 159
ON THE WAGON 159
OPENING HOURS 161
ORDERING 162
OUTDOOR EATING 164
OVERHEADS 168

PASS 170
PEOPLE 170
PIZZA 171
PLAT DU JOUR 172
POP-UPS 173
PRESENTATION 174
PRIZE DINNERS 177
PUDDING 178

QUALITY 181
QUEUING 182
QUOTATIONS 183

REGULAR HAUNTS 186
RESTAURANT GUIDES 187
RESTAURANT REVIEWS 189
RETRO 191
ROMANCE 192

SAUCES 196
SEASONAL FOOD 196
SELF-SERVICE 198
SERVICE 198
SHARING 204
SMOKING 205
SOFT OPENINGS 206
SOLO DINING 207
SOMMELIERS 208
SPANISH 210
SPECIAL REQUIREMENTS 211
SQUEEZED MIDDLE 212
STAR CHEFS 213
STEAK 215
SUNDAY ROAST 217

TABLES 219
TAKEAWAY 221
TEA 222
THEATRE RESTAURANTS 223
THEFT 224
TIPPING 225
TRAVEL EATING 226
TWISTS 230

UNUSUAL 232

VALENTINE'S DAY 235
VALUE 236
VEGETABLES 237
VEGETARIAN AND VEGAN 238

WATER 243
WEDDINGS 244
WINE LIST 245
WORLD'S 50 BEST
RESTAURANTS 247

X-FACTOR 249

YOUNG PLACES 251

ZIG-A-ZIG ... AH! 255

INTRODUCTION

Here is the book for everybody who eats out – and that means you. Because we all of us do it now, whether far too rarely, pretty regularly all things considered, or else so very damned often that sometimes we wonder how ever we manage to get anything done. Oh yes, eating out: it's what each and every one of us is busy getting up to, these days. Speaking for myself, well – lunch and dinner in restaurants are the nearest I ever get to practising any kind of formal religion, and assuredly I am a most devout observer. And not by any means simply because I write a weekly restaurant review: Lord, no – I've always been like that. But this book is not only for experienced old hands who just love to eat out; it is also for those more occasional diners who feel they might like to know a little bit more about it all, to explore its unwritten subtleties, mysteries, contradictions and often perfectly laughable pretensions. You by no means have to be an epicure (in fact, on the whole, it's probably better if you aren't); you don't even have to be that much of a foodie, and certainly not a wine connoisseur – though it surely won't hurt, should you happen to be either thing.

This book is not actually primarily concerned with food and cooking (while both, clearly, are utterly central to the entire gorgeous exercise), and nor is it just another guide to restaurants (although these are constantly alluded to). Simply, we have here a distillation of all you have ever experienced, for good and ill, at the hands of a restaurateur, as well as everything else you really do need to know – every joyous (or otherwise) aspect of the actually rather lovely business of eating out, in a simple A–Z format. It is perfectly possible to read the whole thing alphabetically from start to finish (and, I hope, with pleasure and amusement), or else do feel quite free to let rip and indulge in the very *raison d'être* of an A–Z, by dipping in at will. You will find here all that you hope for and expect, together with a very great deal more besides – each entry treated with affection and humour, although always entirely realistically, and set within a bedrock of fact.

This, then, is the book for people who absolutely understand that the entire experience of eating out – the way, after all, you have chosen to spend your increasingly valuable leisure time and leisure money – is supposed to be about simple enjoyment, friendship and personal indulgence. There are neither rules nor instructions here, but rather plenty of guidelines, suggestions, cautions, advice, trade secrets and the accumulation of maybe rather too much personal experience. A smorgasbord, some might say – a temptingly presented and lavish buffet, crammed with all that ever you could require! Well yes … some might indeed be moved to say that, I suppose, but it's a little rich for my taste. And if you imagine for a single moment that now I am about to sign off this little intro with a cheery 'Bon appétit!', then I'm afraid I have to tell you that you are very woefully mistaken. Do dig in, though …

ALL-YOU-CAN-EAT BUFFET

These tend to be oriental. One wouldn't really care to be more specific than that: let us, shall we, call the food generic – although such buffets did originally spring up in Chinatown, and rather took off from there. Some exist now that offer all sorts of 'cuisine': Chinese, Japanese, Mexican, Indian, Thai, Italian ... which is awfully handy for the more undiscerning yet curious among us who finally can discover what a spag bol might taste like with the judicious addition of some sushi, tacos, chow mein and maybe just a ladleful of vindaloo. All such places are very popular in university towns, fairly naturally, as the student is a questing creature who is constantly seeking to satisfy his appetite with just about anything really, in return for as little money as possible (the overwhelming bulk of his loan, rather obviously, being earmarked for the pub). These places are more than generous with the rice and noodles, as rice and noodles are cheap, and fill you up fast. They do make money, though – despite the seeming impossibility of the bargain on offer – because for every gourmandizing semi-professional who daily attempts with reasonable success to consume at least his own bodyweight, a dozen more people will be quite contented with a merely rational portion. These are called women.

See also: **BARGAIN LUNCH, CARVERY, CHINESE, FUSION**

AMUSE-BOUCHE

The *amuse-bouche* is on the march. It used to be so very rarefied a thing, rather seldom seen, but these days it can attack you from all quarters, and often when you are least expecting such an encounter. It will manifest itself either as a mark of pretension on the part of a so-so restaurant rather rashly attempting and failing to quite make the leap on to the tailboard of a fast-moving bandwagon (and in such an establishment, you will not wish to eat whatever it is they have chosen to present), or, more probably, as a splendid opportunity for a first-class restaurant to do a little bit of flaunting, which is, after all, one of the perks of the job. The *amuse-bouche* (*amuse-gueule*, the other French term denoting an appetizing little nibble, seems rather to have fallen into desuetude) translates as something to tickle the ravenous palate – a cheeky and throwaway little *jeu d'esprit*. Restaurants boasting two and three Michelin stars, or those that earnestly aspire to so dizzying a status, now seem to think that a couple of these to kick off with, and at least a couple more further down the line, will just about do the trick. Such largesse can easily be overdone, sometimes to the point where one has to ask oneself exactly how much raw amusement just the one mouth may decently be expected to bear.

Quality, as ever, will vary – as does desirability. Favourite of both restaurateurs and diners seems to be a 'cappuccino' of soup: a nice little beige and frothy concoction in a shot glass, hot or cold, and, with a bit of luck, charged with an intensity of flavour. Such a thing, if properly made, will always leave you wanting more – as, of course, an appetizer should. Some restaurants will go to enormous bother, filling such as razor shells (ridiculously long and narrow) with little chopped bits of shellfish amid meticulously shredded flecks of something that is green and mysterious, or maybe the jauntiest ribbon of thick and speckled sauce. Such deft creations must take twenty times as long to construct as to devour; indeed, often the waiter will still be indicating with his pinky and holding forth upon the technique and ingredients long after the little frippery has been slipped between the lips and swallowed whole. Upmarket Italian restaurants will give you things you really do want to eat: curls of prosciutto, thin and twisted Parmesan grissini, deep-fried risotto balls, the ubiquitous olive (of which beware – it will ruin your champagne or dry white, should you be sipping one of these). Then, of course, there is the humble and somewhat lumpish bruschetta: chopped tomato and other bits on hefty circles of bread that is either toasted and left to cool, or else plain stale (it is sometimes hard to tell). Far from being any sort of

A French engraving dating from 1886 depicting something
you might think yourself perfectly capable of downing by way of
a very elaborate *amuse-bouche*, should you be feeling inordinately brave.
Either it is that, or else a weapon of war.

canapé or nibble, these strike me as more of a poor-man's snack, which actually fall down in their primary intention in that they are appetizing to neither the palate nor the eye, while being far more filling at this initial and wonderfully anticipatory stage of the meal than you actually would require.

More little delights will arrive just before the pudding, and this can be vexing – either because the last thing you ever really want before pudding is another little pudding, or else because it could well be based upon the same ingredients as the very pudding you have already ordered. And how are you supposed to know? Well you won't know, ever – because restaurateurs delight in such theatrical sleight of hand. From their point of view, the diner's ideal reaction upon being presented with a pre-pudding pudding is the smiting of the brow while simultaneously exclaiming with considerable brio, '*Mon Dieu! Quelle surprise!*' before breaking into a spontaneous and heartfelt round of applause. And before said pre-pudding, you may well be offered such as a mini sorbet (a palate cleanser, for all you out there with perfectly filthy palates); and following the pudding itself, chocolates, petits fours, crystallized fruits … the generosity is all rather heart-warming, really. Some of the very best places will, for favoured regulars or following a celebratory meal, go so far as to press into your hand a small box of truffles, or similar: a going-home present, as if to reassure themselves that at last you are full, and also a tangible expression of their desolation that finally you are leaving (ho ho).

APERITIF

Famously, Kingsley Amis cited the most depressing question in the English language as being, 'Shall we go straight in?' Because before the *amuse-bouche*, one used always in the old days to enjoy an aperitif – something by way of being a bracer. Or a stiffener. But always the point of the thing was to hone the appetite on a strop, hence a sharpener (though Kingsley also said that, in his experience, the only desire an aperitif set up in him was simply for a further aperitif). Be warned: a gin-and-tonic will not do this. Nor will whisky. They both of them dull the palate; and if you have a couple (as gin-and-tonic and whisky drinkers are highly prone to), then gradually, and very soon rapidly, the spirit begins to supplant altogether the desire for food, as any veteran of old Fleet Street can (just about) babblingly testify (although having said all that, if you want a couple of gin-and-tonics or whiskies, then for God's sake have them). An alternative with backbone, however, is the classic dry martini, which somehow seems to achieve the anticipatory tingle that the gin-and-tonic fails to, and this may well be the tickler of your dreams – though only order it in an establishment that you have come to know and trust, or else one whose reputation precedes it: for one man's martini is another man's mess. You must assume that the bar is capable of making one as dry and as cold as possible – i.e. a drop or two of vermouth will have been briefly swilled around the glass amid crushed ice, which is rapidly discarded before the addition of a double measure of high-proof gin from the freezer. Gordon's, which used to be the classic choice, is now rarely favoured among the cognoscenti due to its alcoholic diminution. Beefeater, Bombay Sapphire and Tanqueray are currently the most admired, along with the raft of recent shockingly cool and trendy new ones, such as Hendrick's and Sipsmith, most of them in weird and thoroughly sprauncy bottles.

Vodka? Depends upon what you add to it, if it's a true aperitif you are after. The vodka martini is obviously okay (but please – no embarrassingly leaden asides in a lisping Scottish accent as to its having been either shaken or stirred), though the addition of fruit juices will be very much according to taste. A Bloody Mary is enduringly popular, although unless you are bravely (and probably optimistically) attempting to chase away the gastric and cerebral misery occasioned by all the fun and frivolity of the night before, it can strike one as a bit of a meal in itself (and particularly if they've gone to town and jammed it full of celery). A chilled fino sherry still discreetly bobs about the borders of fashion: neither in nor out, though steadfastly refusing to leave the party.

If there is no separate bar to the restaurant, and neither a dedicated drinks list, you may not know the cost of your aperitif until the bill arrives at the end of the meal ... and it can be something of a shock – one of the ways a restaurant seeks to up its turnover, of course. This is particularly true in the case of champagne, to my mind the perfect aperitif – and in an ideal world Krug or Bollinger, though neither are the ripe bubbles bursting in a flute of Pol Roger, Moët or Veuve Clicquot to be sneezed at (Cristal and Dom Pérignon being best left to ostentatious revellers, who may even inadvertently squirt some in your general direction). The most alluring sight is the gleaming trolley being trundled towards you, surmounted by a vast and silver tureen filled to brimming with an embarrassment of glistening bottles, each of them a name to reckon with, and known to be sublime. 'A glass of champagne, monsieur? Madame ...?' That is the sommelier's unctuous come-on (and that's okay – it's his job to sell wine, and the more expensive the better). Just know that in the sort of restaurant that goes in for such flamboyant display, the unseen cost (and who is going to be so clunky as to ask?) is likely to be ... considerable. Or, let's face it, eye-wateringly wince-making. But look – if you're in such a restaurant in the first place, you can probably manage to swallow both the bubbly and the bill. He will, of course, come calling again, the sommelier with his trolley (and that's okay – it's his job to chance his luck, and the more intrepid the better), though this is the time to put your foot down: we are talking aperitif here, not some unholy booze-up. And do not worry on his account; he will not be fazed, for already he has the wine list up his sleeve (and that's okay – it's his job to press home his advantage, and the more persuasive the better).

See also: BILL, CHAMPAGNE, DRINKING, LIQUID LUNCH, SOMMELIERS, WINE LIST

ATMOSPHERE

'Great atmosphere!' You will often hear people saying that – even restaurant reviewers will say it (and they are not people, not really, not in context), and you've very probably said it yourself on more than one occasion. Yes, but what exactly does it mean? Well, it can mean all things to all men, of course – which is why in the first place we tiptoe around the thing with so very airy-fairy, mealy-mouthed and ethereal a term for it. What are you after? Buzz? Romance? Peace and quiet? Professionalism? The odour of permanence and tradition, this made heady by a top note of money? Restaurants can be all of these, and more – but there is one thing you will know the moment you walk into a place, and that is whether or not its particular atmosphere is to your imme-diate liking, whatever it is that the proprietor might have been striving for. The eateries for which we reserve our most scath-ing judgement, however (and long before we have even so much as sampled the food), are those we perceive as having 'no atmos-phere at all'. By this we generally tend to mean bland, pale, cheaply furnished, windowless, too bright, too dark, *meh* … and empty, devoid of both character and people – save, perhaps, for that lone and miserable outcast of a restaurant reviewer way over there in the far corner, scribbling in a notebook, masticating dutifully (and he's not a person, not really, not in context).

See also: BRASSERIE, BUZZ, COMFORT, DECOR, RESTAURANT REVIEWS, ROMANCE

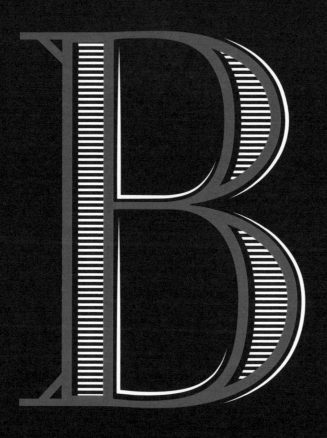

BAR

Britain is still (just about) the domain of pubs. A bar more often than not used to mean one of the shabbier of these corner boozers that had fallen on hard times and been converted on a shoestring into what the proprietors were now pleased to christen a 'wine bar', the decoration comprising row upon row of empty dusty bottles, the ends of wooden wine cases nailed to the wall, a display of dummy champagne magnums and an ice container or so (no one knew why, and nor did it absolutely have to be in the form of a pineapple, though most often it was); the more select might run to a barrel with a spigot in it, this adorned with a bunch of plastic grapes. Apart from one or two chains and a few offshoots of such proper and serious merchants as Corney & Barrow, these bars largely and deservedly have withered on the very vine that once had formed their inspiration. The choice of wine in such places (and particularly by the glass), as well as the knowledge of the staff, were never remotely as broad as one might have hoped for, while always at the same time contriving to be a fair chunk more expensive than ever you expected them to be.

These days, a bar is far more likely to be attached to a restaurant or hotel; and in any decent hotel worth its salt, the bar is liable to be both spacious and comfortable (a good place for an intimate chat, on whatever intriguing subject) while happy to break with pub tradition by actually bringing a drink to your table and running a tab, trusting you not to knock it back and do a runner out of the door. A few hotel bars – such as those at the Savoy or Claridge's, say – have become famous and sought-after destinations in their own right, although normally in a hotel bar what we are dealing with is a staging post: somewhere to sit for a bit before or after a meal. Sometimes, too, it is a place where you can also eat, the term 'bar meals' covering a very wide territory from the tempting to the dire, though the general assumption is that the 'platter' you get here will be light, rapidly served and (you must pray to God) utterly fresh and simple.

The bar attached to a restaurant is a rather different animal. Here you will not, fairly obviously, be receiving food – save for crisps, nuts, olives, pretzels, Twiglets and any other inordinately savoury thing they can conjure in order to lay waste to your appetite and generally pretty much guarantee that the orders for drink will just keep on coming. Often, the bar will be no more than a token couple of tables or a stool or two in front of a shelf, sometimes in a dark and forgotten corner, or even on a different floor from the restaurant altogether. On one thing you must be clear, however: you sit here only if you wish to, and not because you have been instructed so to do. If you have booked a table in the restaurant and have arrived on time, you should not be directed to the bar simply because of the establishment's own inefficiency. If your table is not ready, you have a choice (the paying customer always does have a choice, a truism that is sometimes forgotten by punter and caterer alike). You may squat in the designated cubbyhole with a drink you may not particularly want while consuming handfuls of crunchy and salty things … or else you can walk: there are plenty of other places.

In the larger and more modern sort of brasserie, often the bar will be a grand and glittering affair with comfortable high stools and professional barmen, and this can span the entire and increasingly colossal width of the dining room proper. These are generally very jolly places to be, with lots of interest all around you – should you be a people- and restaurant-watcher, as I am. Just always be sure that the bar is where you have chosen to sit, that's all: never let it be the place where you have been put.

See also: APERITIF, BRASSERIE, CHAMPAGNE, DRINKING, FRONT OF HOUSE, LIQUID LUNCH, SERVICE, SOMMELIERS, WINE LIST

It may or may not be true that there is no such thing as a free lunch (well, come on: of course it's true – we all know that) but bargain lunches abound. However: there is a bargain lunch … and then there is a bargain lunch. People will often tell you of this wonderful place, a real find, a snip, an absolute 'bargain', when all that they mean is that it is merely cheap. Now cheap can just about be okay … if your lunch is pleasant, wholesome, well-cooked, nicely served to you in conducive surroundings, and altogether an enjoyable experience. But ask yourself: how can such a thing be cheap? Overheads are positively crippling these days, so something's got to give. Either the ingredients will be of a very poor standard, or it will be thrown with contempt in your general direction, or else there will be insufficient food on your plate to satisfy a particularly tiny starling whose stomach has been stapled (and often all three). Here is no bargain. Similarly, some establishments will tout what at face value appears to be a very reasonable all-in price, but on closer inspection the menu will be seen to be littered with all these perfectly maddening 'supplements' (particularly for cheese); and apart from subverting the very idea of a set-price lunch, it generally turns out to mean that the meal you actually want to eat will end up costing a whole lot more than the initially quoted figure. What you really have to do is ferret out the very best places serving the very best food (yes, literally) at a bargain price – a similar approach to shopping for 'designer labels' in Bond Street during the sales (should ever you be minded to do such a thing).

There is a reason why this entry is entitled 'Bargain lunch' and not 'Bargain meal'. In the evenings, known and sought-after restaurants will generally be easily filled (and if this is not the case, then they cannot be long for this world). But lunchtime is a different matter – particularly on Mondays and Tuesdays, say, during bitter winter weather or a summer heatwave, when it can be an absolute beast to get the punters through the door. And lo, the set lunch. And yes,

Taking the concept of the 'bargain lunch' to its absolute
extreme – and on a sandwich board, to boot. Clear signs that in
1930s New York, the Great Depression was beginning to, er ... bite.

I know that practically everywhere offers a set lunch these days, but it pays to be discerning. And that usually means a restaurant with a Michelin star, or even two, to its name. In London, the most celebrated lunch deal is at Le Gavroche (two stars), which famously is run and – much more relevantly – cooked in by Michel Roux Jr. For £100, two people receive a couple of *amuse-bouches*, three courses, a bottle of wine and one of water. The china and stemware are of the finest, and all is served impeccably in a legendary and truly charming and elegant room. The downside (well, there just had to be one) is that it is booked up solid for just ever and ever; and if you are not a regular or a 'name' (or know someone who is), then, largely, you have had it. But there are plenty more excellent one- and two-star restaurants offering comparable lunchtime deals – the drawback with these being that while a superb three-course meal can cost as little as £30, the wine mark-ups are usually rather dizzy. But look: they've got to make up the margins somehow, haven't they? In theory, you could call for tap water, and brazen it out. In theory.

See also: BILL, OVERHEADS, QUALITY, STAR CHEFS, VALUE

BILL

The bill: always the least digestible part of the meal, but it simply has to be faced. It sounds rather trite and insultingly obvious to say that you should never go anywhere where the eventual bill is likely to pose a problem, but surprisingly many do, usually in a misguided attempt to impress, borrow money from, sell to, or else seduce their guest – hoping against hope that said guest will not go and plump for the lobster, the Dover sole ... oh and please God not the caviar! And if said guest does indeed turn out to be horribly profligate, the host will order for himself an omelette by way of compensation. This simply will not do: such uneasiness does not make for a relaxing and enjoyable dinner *à deux*. So always go somewhere that is easily affordable, that's the first thing – and then the bill won't leap up and punch you in the gut.

Some restaurants still include a cover charge, which I find very annoying. This used to be imposed in order to take care of the cost of laundering the napery, which was silly enough (it's an overhead: swallow it, or at least disguise it elsewhere – it's rather akin to a taxi slapping on an extra for wear and tear on the tyres), but now it is enforced, and usually by fashionable restaurants, simply because they know they can get away with it. A busy morning-to-night brasserie with a £2-per-head cover charge is going to rake in daily a very tidy pile in exchange for absolutely nothing at all. But don't complain about the cover charge when you see it on the bill; it will have been stated somewhere on the menu, and if you failed to bring along a magnifying glass in order to decipher the grey and diminutive print, that's your lookout. And it is no good moaning about prices: the mark-up on food is huge, but it generally has to be, in order to cover all the unseen expenses, mainly staff. And that is why we most often eat at home.

Sometimes by the end of the meal, the restaurant will rather have lost interest in you, and the very acquisition of the bill can become something of a performance in itself, this involving a degree of self-consciously lukewarm gesticulation and the widening of one's eyes, not to say the miming of the gesture denoting the signing of your name in thin air. It is a strange yet internationally recognized code – strange because nobody, except maybe a resident in a hotel, actually does sign the bill, and nor any more will they be signing a cheque or a credit-card slip; we ought really to be miming the stabbing of buttons, but there has to be a limit to such clumsy tomfoolery. And then sometimes the bill will be presented, whereupon the waiter will quickly throw a few things into a suitcase and emigrate to Australia – as if all you wanted was to marvel privately at the thing's intrinsic beauty, turn it over within your hands, and perhaps even commit it to memory. A word is in order when the bill is placed before

In this illustration from 1930, the lady seems suddenly
and ruefully aware that she really shouldn't have
ordered the caviar, shouldn't have ordered the lobster …
And the gentleman: he is aware also.

you: please return soon with the machine. And it goes without saying that a bill presented before it is actually requested is totally unacceptable, and the sign of a very poorly run establishment.

I do recommend that you check the total – casually, though, and not in the manner of a suspicious and cheeseparing accountant – for it is extraordinary how frequently an extra bottle of wine or an unordered coffee and some side dishes can worm their way into the tally. Of one thing you may be sure, however: the wine, food and coffee that you have actually consumed will never be absent. One embarrassment that can arise when the bill is set down on the table is that chummy little tussle over who is actually going to pay it. Most often it is clear – host/guest, chums who take it in turn – but if not, make a grab for it by all means. Should you counter no opposition, well then you are stuck with it, matey. If two or more people are wrangling, however, keep it short: don't yield too quickly, but make sure that somebody does yield fairly soon, and certainly before the whole thing descends into pantomime – or, worse, fisticuffs.

And finally … a word about *not* paying the bill: contrary to all that you might have heard or seen in films, the restaurant will not have you doing the washing-up. What the restaurant will actually do is call the police, and that will rather be the end of your dining out for quite some considerable while.

See also: OVERHEADS, SERVICE, TIPPING, VALUE

BISTRO

This was such a very buzzy word, back in the 1950s. No one quite knew what 'bistro' meant, though some were darkly suspicious that it might have something to do with the gravy powder of a similar name. It is actually French slang, possibly derived from the Russian word 'bystro' meaning 'quickly'. Which really gets us little further. But back in those innocent days, when eating out well always did pose something of a considerable challenge, it was infinitely more chic to say that instead of a restaurant, snack bar, corner house or cafe … you had dined out in a *bistro*! In recent years they have been making a bit of a comeback, and if you can find an authentic example (which tends to mean that the chef and owner, who may very often be the same person, are thoroughly French and have been there forever), then you should cleave to it – because the combination of authentic quality food and value for money is often unbeatable.

Bistros haven't really changed much over the years, tending to be small and homely, in a throwback and comfortingly rustic sort of a way. The true French peasant classics should all be on the menu: escargots, onion soup, frogs' legs, boeuf bourguignon, coq au vin, onglet frites, cassoulet … you know exactly what I mean. And people seem immensely reassured when enjoying such good and hearty winter fare if they can be sitting on rush-seated country chairs, as famously depicted by Van Gogh, and eating from thick white or brown pottery set on a red gingham cloth, along with a basket of home-made bread, the wine poured out from a *pichet*. And should one be on first-name terms with the owner, and if that gentleman is possessed of a hysterically French accent and may be depended upon not only to welcome you with a hug, but also to wish you 'Bon appétit!' … well then so much the better. We draw the line at striped jerseys, berets and the twiddling of moustaches: we have no wish to play a bit part in a pantomime.

See also: BRASSERIE, FRENCH

BOOKING

Sometimes at the foot of a restaurant listing you might spot the following: 'Booking is essential'. This can merely be a display of overweening and perhaps rather reckless optimism on the part of the proprietor … or, more likely, it means what it says. The most popular and fashionable restaurants are famously booked solid, and something of a closed shop to all but the regulars and celebrities, who have quite a different telephone number from the one you are hopelessly clutching in your sweaty fingers. This favoured elite is constantly importuned, pleaded with to disclose this 'open sesame' number, and of course not one of them will consider doing any such thing. It would be useless anyway, because what happens is that when the privileged person phones, his entire booking history flashes up before the booker on a screen: when last he visited, where he sat, all his preferences, peccadilloes, curious and unnatural demands … whereupon he will invariably be accommodated. I've never worked out quite how they manage it: what if Celeb A wants his usual table, number twenty-five at 8.00 p.m., while Celeb B is simultaneously demanding *his* usual table number twenty-five at 8.00 p.m. …? It's not easy, ensuring the smooth running of such an establishment, not to mention avoiding the ruffling of egos roughly the size of Cornwall. But even these most glittering of places will always hold back a few tables on the off chance that a Hollywood legend, minor royal or rock god might just amble through the door unannounced … and if no such star arrives, then the table could be yours. So do know that you can always just turn up and risk it (though the smaller the party, the better the chance).

On the part of the more determined Everyman, however, it can become something of a mission to acquire a firm booking for a table – any table – in one of these exclusive and much sought-after restaurants. I know of several such establishments in London that daily on the telephone are dealing with the desperate, each of whom is hoping for, say, a table for four at one o'clock for their auntie's birthday three months hence on Friday, 17 May, and is told that, while such a reservation is obviously quite out of the question, no more than two people might just possibly be squeezed into the bar area at 2.45 on Monday, 29 October … whereupon they seize on the offer with babbling gratitude.

But let us for the moment assume that you are sane, and return to the true business of booking. Should the time and date be key to the matter – said auntie's birthday, perhaps, or one of the party just must be away by 3.00 p.m. – then these factors are plainly non-negotiable: simply find the restaurant that can accommodate you, for there always will be one (and not necessarily a hellhole). If, however, Wednesday and not Tuesday will do just as well, and half past one instead of one o'clock is fine, then take the offer, if you want to. In certain places, booking is clearly unnecessary – gastropubs, for example – but otherwise, why take the chance? It's annoying and sometimes a little bit embarrassing to be turned away at the door – and booking is, after all, a completely free service (for the moment, anyway). But having booked, and then finding out later that you can't actually make it after all, it is then quite essential that you phone (preferably) or email to cancel, and particularly so if the table is a large one: for some restaurants, a no-show of six people could mean the difference between profit and loss for the evening. And if you find that you are going to be three people instead of two or five, it is courteous to let the restaurant know – in advance, not when you turn up – so that they have a bit of time to execute a swift re-juggling of the tables. I have heard of some people who routinely book three restaurants for the same time, deciding at the last moment which of them they will patronize. This is odious behaviour in the extreme – and such people will obviously have no truck whatsoever with the new breed of places intended for the young, fashionable and apparently infinitely gullible and impressionable. At these, booking is strictly forbidden: you queue in the sun, you queue in the rain – despite the fact that usually there are plenty of tables inside – this serving the double purpose of making the restaurant appear to be cool and highly sought after, and the person in the queue an absolute idiot.

The other thing you have to be quite clear about is precisely what you are booking: a cosy corner … or the table next to the lavatories? A place on the sunlit terrace … or a couple of stools at the bar? Similarly, should you require something so ghastly as a cake with candles for this blasted mythical auntie who appears to have colonized this little essay, then the time of booking is the moment to make this clear. One other thing that the more in-demand sort of place will do its best to foist upon you is a time limit – most usually for the evenings, when they will hope to sell the table two or even three times over. I personally refuse to have anything to do with such a policy, but it is up to you to decide whether it is acceptable. Should you go somewhere else? Or will one-and-a-half or two hours be sufficient for whatever you had in mind? If so, go for it – but be prepared to stick to the bargain. It's no good at all when your time is up deciding that you'd really rather draw the thing out and order a round of stickies: the next lot of diners will already have arrived – and they booked too. No use, either, chaining yourself to the table, for the restaurateur will saw the leg off. The table's, though – not yours.

See also: FASHION, FRONT OF HOUSE, QUEUING, SERVICE, TABLES, STAR CHEFS, YOUNG PLACES

BRASSERIE

I am rather in thrall to the huge and seemingly unstoppable rise of the fabulous brasserie. The concept of an all-day and often very fashionable eating place where one can scoff and sluice at moderate or huge expense as much or as little as one desires – from 7.00 a.m. to maybe 1.00 a.m. the following morning – within an interior that is a glittering and vaulted palace of marble, mirrors, brass and glass … Oh heavens, this is all so very wonderfully at odds with the old-fashioned and very grisly British way of catering as actually to be quite hysterically funny in its glorious contrasts. Because back in the Dark Ages, the British owners of pubs, cafes and restaurants used to have just the one shared speciality of the house – and that was saying no to most things, while issuing very stern instructions about everything else, and always with grim satisfaction. 'It is half past eight and we've stopped serving breakfast now … Luncheon will not be served until one o'clock on the dot, and we would ask you to be punctual ... It is now a quarter past two and therefore you are too late for luncheon ... The clock has just struck three and so I cannot serve you any further alcohol ... We are serving tea at four o'clock, though regret that you cannot just order tea without something to eat as well ... It is only half past five, and so the bar is not yet open ... Now it is, but I shall have to ask you to deposit your children in the car park ... Last orders for dinner are at a quarter to nine, and please oblige the kitchen by ordering the full three courses in advance from the table d'hôte menu, because no, there isn't an à la carte, and gentlemen are required to wear a jacket and tie ... It is now half past ten so no more drinks may be served, and I must request that you leave now as we are just about to close, and please remember that this is a residential area ...' My God! How did we survive it?

La Coupole in Paris and the great pre-war Austrian cafes are jointly the role models for the modern-day brasserie – La Coupole being truly a staggeringly beautiful room ... although these days that's rather as far as it goes, I'm afraid: the food and 'service' are hardly worth a special journey. That is not the case, however, with the new breed of brasserie, examples of which appear to be opening (in London, certainly) at the rate of practically one every month. They are noisy, but in a good way – because the best and most successful of them, most notably the Wolseley, are always full of happy people. The menus are endless and enticing, the time of day an irrele-vance, and the dress code non-existent – while the general feel is of a non-stop party. You leave, aglow with pleasure ... you return a few weeks later ... and the joint is jumping, the party still in full swing. You can happily eat on your own while pretending to read – or bring a date, hold a celebratory bash, entertain the whole family, close the deal, spot the gaudy celebs and table-hop to your heart's content. The brasserie, quite plainly, is truly everything, to simply everybody.

See also: BAR, BISTRO, BUZZ, DECOR, SERVICE, SOLO DINING, VALUE

BREAD AND BUTTER

'Do you want a roll and butter?' This used to be the ritual question put to a diner in such as a spaghetti or steak house, with nary a mention that it would be charged for. These days we rather expect that bread should automatically be put on the table, or at the very least offered – and a fair variety as well, not just chunks of baguette with all the give and texture of titanium. Some restaurants make rather a big deal of the fact that they bake their own, and it is worth trying out a few variations, as usually they are very good indeed. The danger always is lurking, however, of going all out on a positive orgy of bread, this very much blunting the appetite for the good things to come. It ought to be retained on the table if such as escargots or moules marinière have been ordered, as it will need to be called upon for essential mopping-up duties (some restaurants providing, and some diners requesting, a bowl of superior olive oil solely for this purpose). And then the bread should make a reappearance for the cheese, of course, along with several biscuit alternatives.

In the best restaurants, two sorts of butter will be on the table: salted and unsalted. And they will have been brought to room temperature – and of course are naked and unadorned. The unwrapping of rock-hard little tablets of butter really has no place at the dining table. It's marginally better if it's a circular slab of something from Normandy, say, rather than a silly little industrially produced irritant in foil that you might expect to be thrown in your general direction on an aeroplane – but still you have to go through the business of unwrapping the fiddly thing, and still it will be as cold and unyielding as a mistress in a huff.

See also: CHEESE, ETIQUETTE, SERVICE

Unless they were resident in a hotel, few people used ever to eat breakfast anywhere but home. And people will eat it in hotels because, well – it's something to do, a reason for having risen … though also because it's probably in with the price of the room, and therefore it would surely be morally wrong to fail to exact one's money's worth. And then the best reason of all: it's something of an unfamiliar treat – because although we can't quite keep up with all the latest news from the health front (are eggs okay again now? Has bacon too much salt, but is fine if it's grilled? Do all sausages contain bits of carthorse?), there lingers around the classic fry-up a sizzling aroma of naughtiness, a forbidden feast. And because in hotels these days it tends to be a help-yourself buffet, it follows that one helps oneself to rather too much. And then asks for more toast. And fresh coffee. Justifying the whole shebang with the assertion that one will, after all, hardly be requiring lunch following a breakfast such as this …

The fry-up is both a delight and an Englishman's right – but it has never been cool. It has never been the stylish option. For this, one looks to the suntanned and beautiful men and women on a terrace overlooking the Mediterranean (each probably wearing a pastel cashmere V-neck tied loosely as a shawl about their shoulders), and downing in one their strong *espressi* while toying with a croissant. Cereal will never be cool, but all hotels go through an absolute mountain of it; porridge, too – never the fashionable choice, but gaining in popularity all the time (while yawny old muesli continues to wax and wane).

But to breakfast out in one's own home town … this became the mark of an 'executive', a tycoon, a plutocrat, a fat cat whose days were so thoroughly charged with urgency and busy-ness that 7.30 a.m. was the only possible slot into which they could maybe magnanimously squeeze you. Hence the birth of the 'power breakfast', Lord help us: unsmiling people getting down to the post-dawn nitty-gritty while sipping decaf and tisanes and neglecting to touch the egg-white omelettes that had been specially requested. Then, later still, breakfast became an on-trend alternative to lunching out (as did a posh tea): everyone was doing it – so much so that at the new breed of brasserie it is increasingly difficult to secure a table at even an ungodly hour. But where better to pursue the idea? You want just a single slice of toast? You got it. Steak with hash browns and grits? You got it. Eggs Benedict? You got it. Glass of champagne with that? You got it. A bill as big as the Ritz? You got it.

See also: BRASSERIE, BUSINESS LUNCH, CAFES, CHAINS, GREASY SPOONS, HEALTH AND SAFETY, HOTELS, TEA

BRUNCH

Brunch is an American invention that has caught on terribly well – and which is enjoyed most usually at weekends, for it is by its nature a very drop-of-the-hat, casual and leisurely thing. The word derives, perfectly obviously, from a partial elision of 'breakfast' and 'lunch', while not really denoting an actual fusion of these two meals; after all, one is hardly going to kick off with Weetabix and the lightly boiled egg with soldiers, to follow with a bowl of Brown Windsor and a cut off the joint. Rather, it is a compromise on the times of day when these two meals are traditionally taken – a somewhat doomed attempt at expanding such a concept having been recently made by the highly esteemed Michelin-starred chef Hélène Darroze. She wanted to institute something called 'Le Drunch' – a fusion of lunch and dinner, and eaten somewhere between the customary hours for such fare. Apart from 'drunch' being nonsensical (if anything, it ought to be 'linner'), Mme Darroze should really be told that such an option has existed for centuries: it is called high tea.

But brunch is an occasion perfectly suited to a well-run brasserie with, if required, newspapers to hide behind, and often a minimum of idle chatter ... for, frequently, the bruncher is attempting very tentatively a gradual re-entry into the atmosphere following the mother and father of all nights out. This explains the lateness of the hour and the clammy clutching of a large Bloody Mary, which now, very comfortingly, is just about beginning to work its special magic.

See also: **BRASSERIE, BREAKFAST, LUNCH**

BURGERS

There are many who could one day be in line for an Olympic gold medal in recognition of their peerless prowess in the art of boring you into a coma on the subject of burgers. And we call these people Americans. For here – along with the rather slimy abomination that they have christened the hot dog – is their abiding contribution to the planet's classic dishes: all the world loves a burger, since at its best it truly is a lovesome thing, and certainly the most conveniently grabbable foodie innovation since the sandwich. And just as people from the United States will cherish very fond memories of the diner and the drive-through, so in Britain we will never forget our very first chomping of a Wimpy: that wafer-thin 'patty' between a split cloud of aerated dough, and brought to life by a big rude squirt of ketchup from the squat and very pleasing bright-red plastic tomato.

The burger has come a very long way – indeed, it has conquered the world, cutting with ease through any flimsy barriers such as class, generation, gender and race. And in addition to the many chains devoted utterly to the thing, there are nowadays few more upmarket menus that will not include a variation on the theme. The French, initially snooty (as they continue to be about any comestible whatsoever that isn't actually French), sought to get around the vulgarity of the concept by dubbing it 'steak haché', but really they were fooling no one. And you must never, ever remind them that, outside America, more McDonald's hamburgers are sold in France than anywhere else on earth. And while McDonald's can just about be okay – once in an exceedingly blue moon – there are many far better (though admittedly rather more expensive) options available these days. These include such chains as Byron and Gourmet Burger Kitchen, as well as all the hand-made and sometimes deconstructed varieties in brasseries and restaurants, some of which can cost as much as a steak.

Everyone seems to have within them a story of the day when they ate the perfect, the absolutely 100 per cent perfect burger: oh, the juiciness, the hint of pink at its centre, the just-so degree of its charring, the lightness of the bun, that bite of gherkin, the oozing of the cheese, the tang of mustard and ketchup … Yes, and you must fervently pray that within them is where the story remains. Because, you see, it's one we've heard before.

See also: BRASSERIE, CHAINS, FRENCH, STEAK

BUSINESS LUNCH

You don't hear quite so much about the business lunch as you used to. 'Executives' would ritually and with a perfectly straight face tell their stay-at-home wives that they were in back-to-back meetings all day long, these only briefly punctuated by a short and essential 'business lunch' into which they had been strong-armed – this to make clear that there was not the slightest element of pleasure or relaxation here: it's all just non-stop slog, slog, slog. Same story with 'a quick drink after work with a client'. All nonsense, of course: these were the much-anticipated highlights of the day, drawn out for as long as possible and quite possibly culminating in a visit to Stringfellows – though at the same time more often than not the only occasions when their time was actually employed constructively. You can achieve a very great deal by the time the coffee arrives, following on from fine food and a bottle or so of something decent. And in the old days of repeated rounds of brandy and cigars … well! Mountains were moved, and planets conquered. Because a properly conducted business lunch in the right sort of restaurant actually does *work* – whereas at an office meeting, where everyone will idly twiddle their pens and glance periodically at their winking mobiles while pretending to respect the others' quite wildly divergent viewpoints, the only resolution can ever be the tabling of yet another bloody meeting.

But these days we have become rather coy about the unstated purpose of such a lunch. Well business, of course business; but now its dark and lucrative intent must be veiled in the chiffon of peer camaraderie and mutual esteem. The choice of venue says it all: a two- or three-starred Michelin restaurant, and preferably one where the host is known to the maître d', allied with rather good vintages. Such wines can light up the sky in tongues of fire not only the fact that the guest is being taken very seriously indeed, but also – crucially – that there's plenty more where this came from, matey (and not just lucre, but lunches too).

See also: BREAKFAST, DRINKING, FINE DINING, FRONT OF HOUSE, LIQUID LUNCH, RESTAURANT GUIDES, SMOKING, STAR CHEFS

BUZZ

Buzz is the atmosphere that the new and talked-about places particularly aspire to, while all the old favourites are desperate to retain whatever vestiges of it they can. But what does buzz actually mean, apart from the undulating hum of so many voices in animated conversation and the thrum of a busy and well-oiled restaurant? Well, it isn't about that at all; that's hardly more than background noise. A sort of buzz may sometimes be artificially cobbled up by means of a heavy and concentrated media blitz, by advertising (although when is the last time you saw an advert for a restaurant?), or else by deliberately protracted anticipation over some especially hot new opening, the calculated rationing of bookable tables – and that handy old stalwart, the regular presence of (often paid) celebrities. The real buzz, however, is that which resonates within the bosom of the diner who is lucky enough to have got through the door – simply the thrill of just being there among all these other people who are equally very damned pleased with themselves, and excited in their turn to be there with you. Such a vibe is elusive, though if the smoke catches light it can be instantly contagious, and hugely to be desired … because it don't mean a thing if it ain't got that swing.

See also: ATMOSPHERE, BOOKING, BRASSERIE, FASHION

BYO

This stands for 'bring your own', as in bottle – and, rather sadly, you hardly hear of it, these days: it used to be one way of ensuring a relatively cheap night out. There was only ever one reason for its existence: the restaurant, for some reason or another, had been unable to obtain a liquor licence – for the restaurateur has yet to be born who would willingly pass up on the colossal mark-ups (up to 400 or 500 per cent) that are to be had on wine. A few will steer a middle course – this being likely only if they are in some way allied to a wine merchant – by the understandably popular practice of selling bottles at the retail price plus corkage (a charge for pouring and supplying glasses, and this can range from token to extortionate). But if you do come across a genuine BYO, it is worth going to only if (a) the food is known to be plain and at least decent, and (b) you are fairly seriously into wine. This allows you to bring along a bottle that cost you, say, £30, instead of paying £30 for something that is worth maybe only a quarter of that. But if you're simply intending to pick up a £6 bottle from the supermarket on the way, it's hardly worth the bother of carrying the thing.

See also: OVERHEADS, WINE LIST

A coffee bar in 1950s London, with everyone seemingly
desperate to make the cold and frothy dregs of their cappuccinos
endure into the small hours. Note the impenetrable rocks of
demerara, not to say the plant pot in the form of a sputnik.

CAFES

Cafe ... It's become rather hard to define one, these days. The original sense of the word, somewhere you just stop off at for a quick cup of something good and warming, has been somewhat subsumed by certain trendy restaurants styling themselves cafes, when clearly they are nothing of the sort. And then of course there is the ubiquity of the coffee chains: Starbucks, Costa, Caffè Nero – on and on and on they march, the length of every high street in the land. To one largely female sector of society, not to be carrying one of their outsize cartons would be on a par with leaving their mobile at home, or not carting about also a mini bottle of Evian and possibly an oversized tote containing a yapping dog with the size and demeanour of a rat. In one sense, though, these are true cafes: they do at least adhere to the original principle – although they have been collectively and cannily responsible for having rendered a cup of coffee not so much a beverage as the basis for a doctoral thesis. Macchiato, Americano, Mocha Latte ... or might you be up for a supersized Skinny Frappuccino? Some still remember the days when it was black or white, one lump or two – back in the era when a Gaggia would simply hiss at you steamily, whereas now they all seem to shriek like a highly strung woman under considerable duress.

And what about the sandwich shops, those purveyors of fuel to the office-toiling masses who perhaps find it hard to remember the joys of sitting in a restaurant and being served with things that are hot? Are Pret A Manger and Subway cafes? Loosely, I suppose – though the miserly provision of seating in such places marks them out as primarily takeaway facilities: let the gaudy window entice the hungry punter, secure his loot, show him the door. The staff are friendly enough, although you do feel that they each of them has learnt from an identical script at Friendliness School (as, indeed, is the case).

One of the reasons the traditional tea shop is becoming something of a rarity – except maybe in picture-postcard towns and villages and semi-rural tourist hotspots – is that their very hushed and unhurried cosiness (the sonorous clump of the grandfather clock, the tiered and pretty stand of elegantly doileyed dainties, the dozy old cat insinuating itself around your shins) tempted people with time on their hands to linger interminably over just a cuppa and a scone … and believe me, there's no profit in that. The reason why, in a different context, all the stale, cheap and beery 'old-men boozers' have been stripped out and relaunched as pricey gastropubs: that's where the money lies.

See also: CHAINS, COFFEE, FAST FOOD, GASTROPUBS, LITTLE PLATES, TAKEAWAY, TEA

CARVERY

The carvery is an endangered species – though few, I imagine, will truly mourn its passing. In theory, of course, it's a perfectly wonderful idea: all the food you can eat for a reasonably modest set outlay in a large and ornately overblown sort of faded and forgotten ballroom within a hotel whose glory days are long behind it. You are seated, you order a drink, and then you fool around at the salad bar and select a mishmash of green things that you don't really want while loading up with far in excess of your fair share of prawns. Then comes the main attraction: meat! Glorious meat! Carved in front of you by young chaps who all are wearing tall white toques and who therefore must be master chefs to a man, right? Wrong – oh Lordy, how woefully wrong: they're just young chaps in tall white toques who cut up meat.

The joints will have been recooking under the infrared lights for God alone knows how long, the roast potatoes are as cardboard, the greens akin to a variety of pond slime, and the one-size-fits-all gravy on the lines of a wholly artificially reconstituted and gritty oxtail soup. The plates they give you are small in diameter – but seasoned carvery-goers have long ago assimilated such principles of modern architecture as to allow them to build skywards as high as their heart's content. The result is a grotesque amount of food, much of it left. Whereupon the more committed (as many of them should be) will waddle (yes, I'm afraid so) back up to the counter in order to just try the chicken, to just try the lamb, to just try the pork …

Oh dear oh dear. No, we shall not mourn the carvery's passing. Though you must never confuse such places with hotels and restaurants that do a proper Sunday roast, and nor with such a legend as Simpson's-in-the-Strand, where a vast and gleaming trolley will be wheeled to your table (this being rather the point of the place) and pleasingly enormous portions of perfectly wonderful beef or lamb carved for you by a professional (whom you ought to tip as soon as he has done so, by the way, this being quite separate from the overall gratuity for the meal – a couple of pounds per person is about right).

See also: ALL-YOU-CAN-EAT BUFFET, CHAINS, HOTELS, SUNDAY ROAST, TIPPING

CASINOS

No one goes to a casino primarily for drinks – but all of the more stylish examples (should you be perceived to be a reasonably serious gambler) will provide them gratis. And once your taste has been established, more will arrive quite frequently, and usually by way of a beautiful young woman who is soignée in an evening gown, and pretending to like you. If you are anything approaching a 'high roller', a lavish dinner of the 'international' sort (lobster, fillet steak and so on) will also be laid on for you, and quite free of charge. This will turn out to be far the most expensive meal of your entire life on earth, by a factor of ten.

See also: CLUBS, INTERNATIONAL FOOD

CELEBRATIONS

We all understand why you might not wish to hold a special dinner party in honour of a birthday or anniversary at home (the mess, the worry over the menu, the mess, the *placement*, the catering to allergies and vegetarianism, the choices of wines, the decoration, the mess, the mess, the mess), but you ought also to think carefully about quite what it is you expect a restaurant to provide. And having done so, you then might consider a private room. This really is favourite: yes, it's the more expensive option, obviously, but if you're already committed to what is going to cost you more than plenty anyway, you may as well go the whole hog (the whole hog, incidentally – in the form of a suck-ling pig – being a pretty good choice for such an affair as this: it makes everyone go 'Ooh!' and 'Wow!', save, of course, for the inevitable sen-timentalist who will be ostentatiously and volubly sad over the fate of the poor little crispy creature). And in a private room, you can let rip: raucous and maybe even ribald anecdotes, party pieces, a speech or so, a wheeled-in lit-up cake, the cavorting of *die Kinder* … even, Lord help us, a sing-song. Within the restaurant proper, however, you will be inhibited. And if you are not inhibited, everyone else in the room may be relied upon to loathe you most utterly.

See also: CHILDREN, CHRISTMAS, FAMILY MEALS, MOTHER'S DAY, NEW YEAR'S EVE, VALENTINE'S DAY, WEDDINGS

CHAINS

And lo, in the beginning was the Lyons Corner House: opulently fur-nished, sometimes with a little live palm-court music, the 'nippies' tricked out very smartly, just like their counterparts at the Ritz. The next chain to make any sort of a collective impression (it did, at least, if you were aged sixteen or under) was the Wimpy Bar. Then came a bit of a lull until the golden dawning of the Berni Inn, and then the

The way it used to be. But this is not New Year's Eve
in a grand hotel, but just another day at a Lyons Corner House,
during the late 1920s. The orchestra is in full swing –
as is the army of sweetly tricked-out 'nippies'.

Angus Steak House: apparently posh food in an apparently posh set-ting for not apparently posh people. This combination of flattery on the part of the restaurant and the punter's willing self-delusion had rather a lot to do with why they hung around for quite as long as they did; indeed, the latter of them continues so to do. The death knell of both the Angus and the Aberdeen steak houses has been plangently tolled on so very many occasions – but still you will see the perfectly bewildered pair of tourists squatting on the velveteen window ban-quette of the red and radioactively glowing nightmare interior, bright-green paper napkins pertly folded before them just so, while they manfully wrestle with their diminutive rump, the cost of it, and what that works out at in euros.

Berni was more traditionally styled and family-orientated: the big and much-anticipated weekend slap-up feed. Way back in that tender and distant time, grilled steak was seen to be on a par with ambrosia. The diner was eager to be tempted by the gaudily illustrated menu: 'A juicy portion of mushrooms! Go on – treat yourself!'; and, follow-ing the inevitable Black Forest gateau, an Irish coffee. Or a Scotch coffee ... French coffee – any coffee at all, really, so long as it involved a slug of booze, a frothy cloud of aerated and ersatz cream, and a tidy little surcharge. The legacy lingers on with a vengeance in such 'mine host hostelries' as Harvester, Toby Carvery and quite a few more of them, all of which are owned by conglomerates, most of them breweries. They're all right, if that's what you want.

But most of the high-street chains are unashamedly middle-to-downmarket. McDonald's is the most obvious example, but there are meandering legions of others, each having carved out a recogniz-able brand-led niche for itself: tapas, tacos, chicken, burgers, pasta, whatever – most of them occasionally okay, if you are on an extremely tight budget and are in a very great hurry indeed. Then there are the 'oriental' ones, such as Wagamama, and those others revolving (liter-ally) around a ceaselessly trundling conveyor belt (this, for me, taking the concept of food from a manger a step too close). Café Rouge has for an unconscionably long while attempted to be all things to all men, while consistently failing to be anything whatsoever to absolutely anyone at all. The new, rather sprauncy breed, such as Côte, is much more the thing – though you could be surprised to know that there are far more chains than you might actually be aware of, because individual restaurants, although owned by a corporation, are cannily never 'branded', but left as stand-alone entities with completely different names and frontages. They are seen to be unique, but it is not hard to spot the many layers of overlap, particularly within the outposts of the ever-growing empires of Richard Caring (the Ivy, J. Sheekey, Le Caprice, Balthazar – loads more) and Jeremy King and Chris Corbin (the Wolseley, the Delaunay, Colbert, Brasserie Zédel, etc.). All of these, by the way, are pretty much uniformly excellent, just not quite as individual as you may have believed.

See also: BRASSERIE, BURGERS, FAMILY MEALS, STEAK

CHAMPAGNE

Although this eternally delightful essence of effervescence is frequently and joyously alluded to within the scope of other entries, it somehow seemed rather rude not to bestow upon champagne its own little private VIP niche, cordoned off by an unsmiling bouncer, his hand quite steady on the velvet rope. It has become increasingly usual to kick off lunch or dinner with a glass of bubbles (and, I happen to think, it is the perfect way to round them off as well). Prosecco and French sparklers from such areas as the Languedoc are very acceptable and currently fashionable alternatives, Cava for some reason very much less so. The new popularity for fizzy things is very good news for the restaurateur, for the mark-up can of course be sensational. Do know what you are ordering, though: many 'house' champagnes are the ones that you avoid in the supermarket because (a) you have never heard of them, and (b) the label is perfectly vile.

Many ordinary generic champagnes are released when still far too 'green', but anyway are of the sort of standard that even with a couple of years' bottle age under their belts are never really going to amount to much; in such cases, a decent Prosecco will be by far the better bet, and cheaper too. But many superior restaurants will offer you the rare opportunity to savour a glass of something possibly vintage that you may not run to at home, and of which you would not consider ordering a whole bottle in a restaurant. Moët & Chandon has come on leaps and bounds, and is really quite lovely (pronounced 'mow-ett' and not 'mow-y', by the way: the name is Dutch). And Pol Roger ... always a treat. As to Bollinger and Krug, well – need one say more?

A word about flutes: some are bountiful and invitingly generous, others decidedly not – and these tend to be the standard miserable little cheap things that aren't even filled to near the brim (champagne being the one exception to never filling a glass to near the brim). With some rather sprauncy flutes, the champagne descends into the very stem itself, this meaning only that your hand will warm up this part of the beverage, rendering it claggy and therefore undrinkable. Saucer glasses (like those made famous about a hundred years ago by Babycham, and reputedly formed upon the breast of Marie Antoinette – and if this is true, she must really have been a terribly flat little thing) have lately been making an ironic comeback; restaurateurs approve wholeheartedly, because their capacity is pitifully small. Oh, and don't ever think of downing one of these wacky little saucers too quickly, as the bubbly will assuredly bypass the mouth and course down the length of your jowls.

See also: APERITIF, BAR, DRINKING, SOMMELIERS, WEDDINGS, WINE LIST

These are very showy affairs – and the participants would have it no other way. Usually black tie, with the jewels taken out of the safe for the night, and usually in the ballroom of a superior hotel (which will have been persuaded to reduce its rates dramatically because … it's for charidee!). Tables are sold for some or other dizzying sum, and these will be peopled by those who are known to support very generously an array of worthy causes (i.e. are rich). The food will be beautifully presented, instantly forgettable, and not remotely the point. Then comes the auction. Do not ever attend one of these shindigs if you naively assume that the price of your place and that of your guests is in any way a conclusion to the matter: this is merely the hors d'oeuvres – for now you are expected to dig deep, the auction being the meat and potatoes of the thing. This will be conducted by some or other publicity-dependent and maniacally extrovert clown who may in some way vaguely be associated with the cause in question, but anyway must certainly be recognizable from television. All sorts of things will be auctioned – not generally actual objects (unless handbags, stage cos-tumes or even items of lingerie donated by the famous because … it's for charidee!), but more usually such as a dinner for four at a restaurant of considerable reputation, a stay on an oligarch's yacht, lunch with a star, a week at a health farm or (increasingly, these days) an unpaid internship in a glossy and high-profile media outlet for one's gormless and spoilt-rotten offspring, prior to their decamping to finishing school, or else a cushy billet with a wine merchant, wangled through chums.

The grinning and cackling emcee will cavortingly delight in exact-ing extraordinary sums from the diners, who in turn are perfectly thrilled to be seen by all to be able to afford with ease quite lunatic amounts of money for things they certainly don't need, and hardly even want. Because … it's for charidee!

A postscript: the waiting staff and back-room boys are very approving of such events because male guests drink, and female guests don't eat – a subtle distinction, but one that anyway results in a positive mountain of leftover very posh pickings.

See also: BUSINESS LUNCH, CORPORATE ENTERTAINING, FORMAL DINNERS, HOTELS, PRIZE DINNERS

CHEESE

....

Although the custom has rather fallen away, just lately (maybe to do with diets, maybe to do with health), a cheese course always used to form the traditional rounding-off to a good lunch or dinner – although in France, of course, they serve it before the pudding. This is the right way round, in my view, but not, as many believe, because then one may polish off the red wine. Red wine doesn't actually go terribly well with most cheeses, and adds very little to any of them; certainly, with such as a Stilton, say, you'd be far better off with something like a Sauternes. But at whatever stage of the meal you choose to eat your cheese, you really ought to know the calibre of the restaurant before you even bother with the trouble of ordering it. Are they offering 'a selection'? Best avoided: you will be served with three mean little triangles of palely loitering anonymity, fresh from the fridge. What you want is a proper trolley, with someone in charge of it who knows what they are talking about: when you say, 'What's that orangey one over there?' you require a knowledgeable answer.

On a trolley, the cheese is very likely to be in condition – that is to say, brought gently to room temperature (not sweaty and oozing, though certainly not cold either). If you would like rather more of one variety than has been sliced for you, ask for it: it will not be refused. And there is no sight more gratifying than an actual small truckle of Stilton wrapped in a linen napkin (these days, alas, seen only in a very few traditional restaurants and gentlemen's clubs), a nice gooey gobbet of which may be gouged out for you. In addition to celery, grapes and maybe even a fig or so, oatcakes and Carr's

Table Water crackers should always be available, along with whatever other biscuits – and, of course, fresh bread – the establishment might care to offer. Even after a damn good meal, a well-stocked cheese trolley is hard to resist, but do try not to ask for more than you can eat (remembering, if pudding is yet to come, that, well … pudding is yet to come). Sharing a selection with others at the table is always a rather chummy option; and do be aware that if you are enjoying a set lunch, there is almost always a supplement for cheese – and it can be hefty.

Cheese can also come in the form of a savoury, such as a rarebit. These can be a delight, though maybe only after a lightish meal, and in place of both cheese and pudding. That said, should you wish to follow a savoury with a wedge of cheddar and a bowl of blancmange, then by all means do so: it's pleasure, after all, that we are pursuing here.

See also: **BARGAIN LUNCH, PUDDING, WINE**

CHILDREN

Some establishments simply adore to be utterly overwhelmed by all the joy of gay and babbling children. These are called Italian restaurants. Others, however, can be rather more circumspect, often discouraging – if not outrightly banning – any ickle sweethearts who still are of an age where they might feel inclined to run around madly in circles, make faces at other diners, roar maniacally and throw food (not French children, then). This will make for a hellish occasion for everyone in the room – everyone, that is, except the doting parents, who will view their offspring's lovably free and unfettered spirit with nothing but a warm indulgence. Such parents ought by now to have learnt that these blasted kids of theirs would really be so much happier excitedly extracting the toy from a Happy Meal in McDonald's, and that's where the little blighters should bloody well be.

And don't get me on to screaming babies …

See also: **FAST FOOD, ITALIAN**

CHINESE

There are Chinese restaurants ... and then there are Chinese restaurants. The average high-street set-up, which almost certainly will double as a takeaway, can sometimes be a useful port of call for relatively inexpensive, relatively flavoursome, very filling (thanks to all that MSG) and generally rapidly served fodder. The food was long ago tailored to British taste – or, as the Chinese would laughingly insist, lack of it. We like nothing better than to chow down on chow mein and special egg-fried rice and Peking duck and fried seaweed and sweet-and-sour anything, preferably all on the same plate. In such places that specialize in selling all this sort of thing, you won't find anything that the British might find to be strange and unnatural (such as, say, chicken's feet – which, I am forced to remark, if you haven't eaten, don't). The interiors can be drab and run down in the extreme, or else a little insane, tricked out in a gleefully gaudy parody of the genre, with much writhing dragon and tasselled lantern in teeming and colourful evidence.

Chinatown used generally to be seen as the benchmark, the authentic destination ... but, in truth, it has long ago succumbed to catering to tourists and impoverished students staying alive by way of the all-you-can-eat noodle bar. But, you might point out, these restaurants are full of Chinese people! Always the mark of a good one, right? Well no, not really: would you recommend a branch of Greggs because it was packed with the British, hunkering down with a sausage bake? No – the reason these places are full of Chinese people is because they are pretty cheap, and the area (being Chinatown) is full of Chinese people, so where else are they going to go? And – in passing – a word about chopsticks: many people seem to derive a tremendous kick from demonstrating how very deft they are with these tricky little devils. See them twinkling about between their fingers, ever capable of picking out even a single little grain of rice! Yes, and then there are the others who appear to be attempting to crochet with just the one badly crippled hand: bean shoots and peas are sent skittering out in all directions save that of their mouth. Do not inflict such gross ineptitude upon your fellow diners, who by now are perfectly sick of ducking down and shying away from flying gobbets of black bean sauce: either learn to control your chopsticks, or, if that strikes you as just too much faffing about, request a fork. There is no shame in this. The fork is a fine invention; indeed, some may look askance at a continent that, in the face of two thousand years of relative modernity, persists in horsing around with a couple of twigs. And, while we're at it, a word in passing about Peking duck: these are those burnished mahogany things that so often are displayed in the windows of the more authentic joints. That they are probably made of plastic and have been dangling there for decades is neither here nor there: the real thing is gorgeous when shredded, no doubt about it … but the so-called pancake that you are supposed to construct around it is no such thing, being cold, more akin to parchment and utterly devoid of flavour. The gloop of industrial soy sauce forms a horribly credible glue, to which must then adhere silly little strips of cucumber. Well, you really must ask yourself: why on earth …? Just eat the duck, is my advice: it's very good with but a few fried noodles.

There are other places, however – the very select few – that are perfectly sublime: among the very best restaurants you can get, and with prices as high as you like. The food here will be always the real deal: not sweet and sour, nor obliterated by soy. What's more, the waiting staff are likely to be smiling, efficient and polite – in hilarious contrast to the infinitely lesser establishments, where the staff are very often visibly put out by your effrontery in having walked through the door in the first place. No hint of inscrutability here: they hate you.

See also: ALL-YOU-CAN-EAT BUFFET, INDIAN, SERVICE, TAKEAWAY

CHIPS

Chips have come rather a long way since the days when they were more or less exclusively pale and yellow foldable things that came with a chunk of battered cod or rock salmon in a greasy paper bag from a 'chippy', and dowsed in Sarson's vinegar. Although that can be nice too – and particularly late at night when you're absolutely starving and everywhere else has closed. But fish-and-chip shops now can really be very good indeed: they garner awards.

Chips in restaurants – essential with a steak, of course – may be broadly divided into fat and thin. The fat, these days, will generally be described as 'hand-cut' and very likely 'triple cooked', a worthwhile if time-consuming process that involves the constant ridding of excess fat and starch between each operation. This will result, ideally, in a lovesome golden thing that is dry and crisp on the outside (with no glutinous traces of whatever it was fried in – preferably goose fat or beef dripping) and wonderfully floury within. 'Wedges' are a variation, but these can tend to be unpeeled, which you either care for or you don't (I don't). Then there is the thin: frites, or French fries. More often than not, these are bought in, in vast frozen sackfuls, and then fried either well or indifferently; they can be all right, but generally are wilting and flaccid, way over-salted and really rather pointless. They cannot compare with freshly prepared frites, deep fried in the hottest oil and patted dry.

Do beware the dining companion (usually female) who never orders chips because of the calories, but will 'just have one of yours …'. And then eats the lot. Such a person is equally likely to have given up cigarettes, but will 'just have one of yours …'. And then smokes the lot. *See also*: FAST FOOD, FISH, STEAK

Christmas comes earlier and earlier every year, as all of us can hardly be unaware. Harrods sets up its festive department in August because they say that foreign (and particularly American) tourists like to buy box-loads of Christmas-tree baubles with 'Harrods' inscribed upon them in green and gold glitter (and if this is true, as I suppose it must be, then I shall retire to Bedlam). And as early as September it is not unusual to see cards on the tables of the kinds of restaurant that put cards on their tables, these – amid cartoons of Santa, robins and jingle bells – enquiring of you brightly: 'Have you booked your Christmas special meal with us yet?'. Well, let me see now ... um – no, in fact I haven't; and nor, very obviously, shall I. Ever. Because you really don't want to be in restaurants very much in December, you know: it's when restaurants are given over to the amateurs. Tables will be shoved together for an office 'do'. Crackers will be evident. Maybe even balloons and (oh dear God, please spare us) 'party poppers'. Duane and Hayleigh from Sales could well become rampant – as inflamed as the trolleyed-in Christmas pudding. And the 'special menu' will be what, do you think? Yes indeed: turkey and stuffing and cranberry sauce, not to forget 'all the trimmings'. Which is, of course, exactly what you are intending to eat – though a highly superior version of it – within the peace of your own home, come the twenty-fifth ... so why ever would you want it now?

If the faff of Christmas Day itself is rather beyond you this year, then you might consider letting a restaurant take the strain – though for your own sake, make it somewhere really good: this is no time for bargain hunting (not, of course, that you'll find such a thing as a bargain). This is where the top hotels really come into their own: such as Claridge's or the Dorchester (and, of course, many others) really do cater the thing magnificently. Expensive? Oh Christ, yes – wildly. But then things are, aren't they, at this oh-so-special time of the year? And you want a happy Christmas, don't you ...? Well then.

CLOAKROOM

A dedicated cloakroom is much to be desired. It is pleasant to be relieved of one's coat, hat, scarf and maybe bags of shopping as soon as one enters a restaurant, and to receive a numbered token so that there won't be any fuss when it comes to retrieving them. Often there will be a prominently placed saucer of one- and two-pound coins. These are intended not – as my son when but a child once so optimistically believed – to be taken, but to be added to. It isn't obligatory – but why not, after all? It hardly adds much to the cost of the meal. And should the attendant actually help you on with your coat (becoming rare, and it shouldn't be), then a tip of a pound or two is rather essential.

The alternative to a cloakroom is always fairly miserable: either you sling your stuff over the back of your chair, or else you abandon it to a Thonet bentwood stand way over there by the door, whereupon you're going to be fretting throughout the meal about the safety of your highly nickable beaver-felt fedora that you have only just that morning bought from Bates the hatter in Jermyn Street. Even worse is a mingy little row of far too few hooks, which necessitates coat being piled upon coat; and when the first to arrive come to leave the restaurant, they must perforce go in for a great deal of unassisted burrowing, delving and excavation, such strenuous endeavours inevitably resulting in your coat, and your coat alone, landing up on the floor.

See also: SERVICE, TIPPING

CLUBS

Clubs – by which I mean private members' and gentlemen's clubs, not those of the night, strip or gambling varieties – fall into just the two categories: those of which you yourself are a member, and those to which you are invited as a guest. Your own club really ought to be a home from home, somewhere you can pretty much eat what you please at a time of your choosing, alone or in company and sitting anywhere you like. Even so, there are certain niceties to be observed: if there is a communal central club table, whether you are on your own or with chums, it is de rigueur to seat yourself next to the last person to have done so – and not to beetle off down to the far end, there to establish a rump and rival colony. You will be billed for just your own intake, so if you wish, in a flush of bonhomie, to pay for wine, say, for the pair of fellows in your immediate vicinity, make sure that the sommelier is aware of your intentions. And talking of billing: clubs vary in their systems. Sometimes you pay there and then, as in a restaurant – though at the better ones, no bills or credit cards are ever in evidence, the charge arriving usually monthly and exacted either by direct debit or else by way of a straightforward bill. Check it by all means, but pay it quickly. This is not just manners, but also helps you to keep a grip on costs that can so very easily spiral.

Whether or not to belong to a club in the first place is a question in itself. A members' club is owned by its members collectively, and in theory this ought to mean that although the establishment has to make money in order to survive and prosper, the meals are generally cheaper than in a comparable restaurant – although any saving here has to be balanced against the annual subscription, which can be just a few hundred pounds, or else thousands: how often you intend to use the club is therefore a factor. And of course you do know that you can't just march right in and demand to be a member ...? In the best clubs you require a proposer and a seconder before signatures can be gathered from other members: it can take many years to be elected. One notable thing about members of the elite of London clubs is that they all are quite convinced that their club is the finest of all ... Indeed, if this is not the case, then they are in the wrong club.

If you are a guest in an unfamiliar club, you must permit your-self to be guided by your hopefully able host. Almost certainly you will be forbidden – both by club rules and by the *noblesse oblige* of your host – to pay for anything at all, and nor should you offer. The time for reciprocation comes on another occasion, when you invite him to either your own club or a restaurant. Normally a guest will be given a menu without prices – a dying courtesy, but still meticulously observed in the better establishments. It is polite to select from the choices within the set lunch or dinner menu, if there is one (unless you find it actively repellent: we are not going in for self-flagellation here), but otherwise feel free to let rip. In some clubs, however, food is not ordered quite so straightforwardly as that: at White's, for instance, the entire meal is ordered from the sole menu stationed on a lectern, and attended by the head waiter; in the Savile, a pad and pencil are provided at table, whereby you tick off your options – and it is, of course, up to the member host to deal with all this arcana. As a guest, you should not ask for further drink – though if your host is at all up to scratch, you really shouldn't have to. Compliment the club, but of course, although not to the extent of saying that you would just *love* to be a member: this puts your host in an awkward position.

Most gentlemen's clubs now have lady members as well, whose dress is rather up to them. Gentlemen, however, will be expected to wear a suit, or at least a jacket and tie. Trousers as well, of course; let's not be silly. A postscript: should you be a member of the Garrick Club, it is generally advisable not to be sporting the famous salmon-and-cucumber tie in similarly august fellow establishments. They really don't care for it, you know.

See also: BILL, CASINOS, ETIQUETTE

COFFEE

I've always rather wondered how the unshakeable convention for having coffee after a meal initially got up and running, before rapidly assuming so unwavering a grip. And now it's hardly more than a habit, a reflex – because following a good lunch or dinner with water and wine, you don't really want or need a cup of coffee, do you? I mean, not *really*, not like when you crawl out of bed in the morning, able neither to focus nor to articulate, and a shot of caffeine is absolutely essential. Or in the middle of the afternoon, when you pop into a cafe for a latte or something. Admittedly, the aroma of a freshly made espresso is both rich and alluring, even if (in common with Havana cigars) the flavour never quite rises to such magnificent promise. And espresso, obviously, is the only sort of coffee to contemplate, having eaten – not just for its modest proportions and intensity, but also because it goes so terribly well with brandy or malt whisky, should you be so inclined.

The very tininess of an espresso, of course, can often be perfectly ludicrous: sometimes quite literally a spoonful. So a double …? Occasionally, they just add water, you know – though this very much depends upon where you are: a good place won't. And in exchange for this concentrated little heart-jolter, many restaurants are more than happy to relieve you of up to four quid; but all respect to those establishments that do not charge for refreshers (because if they do, it is horribly easy for two people to rack up twenty pounds or more for this little post-prandial indulgence). And why – when you order pudding – do waiters always, but always, ask if you will be wanting coffee afterwards? Why don't they ask you … afterwards? Possibly irrationally, I find this compulsion on their part quite perfectly maddening.

See also: CAFES, TEA

Eating out should be all about pleasure and a certain degree of self-indulgence, so it ought to go without saying that comfort in all its aspects is quite essential. The seating, most obviously – though it is perfectly extraordinary just how many restaurants seem to have gone considerably out of their way to supply to their customers the most bum-numbing and incidentally hideous numbers they could lay their hands on. In fast-food places, this is just about acceptable (they want the punter in and out in record time so that they can give the whole place a jolly good hosing down), but in any restaurant where it is expected that you will dawdle for up to two or three hours, uncomfortable chairs are simply not to be stood for, and nor to be sat upon. More fashionable, 'young' places are increasingly opting for benches broadly on the lines of a bookshelf, and stools designed with pre-school toddlers in mind – and so for that let us all join in roundly damning them to blazes. My own preference is for a chair upholstered on both the back and the seat, and preferably with arms, although one other source of discomfort arises from the chairs being perfectly fine in themselves, while the facing banquettes will be several inches lower, compelling all who sit on them to assume a plaintive expression of meek supplication. This ridiculous disparity is very, very common, and completely mystifying.

The temperature too is important: no draughts, though neither an adjacent fire or radiator simply belting it out. Comfort comes also from the sense that one is in the hands of professionals upon whom one can totally rely: first-rate service, and the knowledge that the correct dish will be promptly served to the appropriate diner, and of course that it will be a joy to eat. Lighting as well: you do not want it as bright as a stage, nor should you tolerate it being as flat and deadeningly lit as a supermarket or car park. Neither can we have it so 'romantically' or 'atmospherically' dark as to lead us to believe that we have very suddenly gone blind, while holding the candle ever closer to the menu in a forlorn attempt to decipher the bloody thing.

You need to be a comfortable distance from the nearest table, this eliminating the possibility of being made uncomfortable by the violence of the ongoing argument, the lowering misery of the relentless grown-up business discussion, or the frankly salacious and unsupportably titillating seduction. You need to be comfortable, too, that the eventual bill will not send you into shock – and perhaps most importantly of all, it is vital that you are thoroughly comfortable with your fellow dining companions: that bit is up to you.

See also: **BILL, DECOR, FAST FOOD, PEOPLE, SERVICE, YOUNG PLACES**

COMPLAINING

If ever you are moved to complain in a restaurant, then already the meal is compromised: it simply comes down to a question of degree. You quickly have to assess the severity of your grievance, and whether or not it can be remedied. So, if more or less immediately upon entering a restaurant you have divined that there will be much to complain about – it strikes you as unappealing, maybe unhygienic, the welcome is unwelcoming, the temperature stuffy or chilly, the table in quite the wrong place, the chairs uncomfortable – it really is as well to just turn around and leave: there are plenty of other places. If, however, once the meal is underway something comes up that is not to your liking, it is up to you to raise the matter immediately, having decided exactly what it is you want to be done about it. For example, if an entrée is cold, do not eat it and then complain to the waiter that it was cold: he hears your dissatisfaction, but can really do nothing about it. So as soon as you have ascertained that your entrée is cold, summon the waiter. Do you want it replaced with another of the same that is hot? Or do you wish not to take the risk but to change the order to something else? Similarly, if the meat is inedibly tough, if something is woefully under- or overcooked, know immediately if you want an alternative. If you gnash your way miserably through food you are not enjoying and then complain afterwards, you have only yourself to blame for the fact that satisfaction will be unforthcoming.

That's your side of complaining; the other element belongs with the restaurant. What you don't actually ever want is an argument of any description: the waiter – or, if he is frightened, obstreperous or non-English-speaking (any or all of which are entirely possible), then the head waiter – must apologize for the offending plate and replace it with either another of a proper standard or else an alternative, as instructed. We do not want him saying that it looks quite all right to him, or that no one else in the restaurant has complained about it. This is equally true of wine: if it is corked, say so (and corked does not mean that there are fragments of cork in it, but that it has reacted badly, is oxidized or is merely tired – anyway unpleasant and certainly undrinkable). It should be whisked away instantly: we can't have a sommelier sniffing it, sipping it and implying with his eyebrows that you don't know what you're talking about (though having said that, it is as well to know what you are talking about). Taste the replacement bottle ... and if it too is corked (this can happen – there are bad batches), send it back again and review your position: a third bottle of the same? Or plump for something different? Many sommeliers in restaurants of a higher bracket obviate the whole charade by taking the simple precaution of tasting the wine themselves before it is offered to the customer: smiles all round.

Sometimes even the best-run restaurant will get things wrong: a dish you didn't order placed before you; a well-done steak when rare was requested. If they make good the error swiftly and with a minimum of fuss, then fine. What they must never do, however, is leave on the table all the unoffending dishes so that the other diners either stare at them wistfully as they grow ever colder, while politely awaiting the arrival of the replacement meal ... or else eat up gingerly, so as not to be finished before the errant plate eventually arrives. And this, of course, is why some people – knowing something to be wrong – will simply not complain: because no matter how you play it, it is going to throw the whole of the table out of kilter. If you are going to point out that something is wrong, however, then for pity's sake do not wait for the waiter's ritual request for reassurance: 'Is everything all right …?' If it is wrong, you do not wait to be asked.

A decent restaurant – and certainly one that knows you – will not charge for the dish that was wrong (even when they have put it right). Some will even waive the price of the entire course for however many people may have been dining. They should at least be offering you a glass of something. A different question arises, though, when there is nothing actually wrong with the food, but simply it is not to your liking. You were maybe ordering recklessly, but now discover that you have been over-adventurous: you just know after the first mouthful that you are not going to enjoy this dish. You could grin and bear it … but, as ever, enjoyment is our quest here, is it not? So best to be honest: summon the head waiter, deliver unto him a precis of the above, and leave it up to him. In a larger and better establishment, they will probably allow you to choose again (and for God's sake be sensible this time), whereas in a more modest set-up, you may well encounter the equivalent of the regretfully shrugged shoulder. You have no automatic right of redress in this case: the ball is wholly in their court.

So, in short: don't nitpick, but do complain when you ought to. Always, however, do this politely but firmly: waiters are not there to be harangued. If, despite all your efforts, satisfaction is not obtained, you can do little except withhold the tip and vow never to come to the restaurant again. You may even, if you like, tell them this upon leaving – though the sort of place that would allow a customer to depart feeling so very bitter and cheated will hardly give a damn.

See also: BILL, COMFORT, FRONT OF HOUSE, INEDIBILIA, MENUS, ORDERING, SERVICE, SOMMELIERS, TIPPING, WINE LIST

CONCEPTS

Concept: dread word. The 'concept' of any restaurant on earth should simply be good food to be eagerly enjoyed, no? And well served in pleasant surroundings …? Well, some of our more toe-curlingly fashionable establishments would strenuously beg to differ. A very bouncy member of staff, probably in a pertinent yet almost certainly asinine costume, will bound across the room, hunker down beside you and announce very brightly right into your face his or her name (almost as if anyone at the table actually gave a damn, or something) and then ask you whether you have dined here before. Whatever the truth of the matter, for pity's sake say yes. Otherwise you will be in for the whole nine yards: endless and excited babble going into the intricacies of how the concept actually *works*, plus all sorts of absolute guff to do with the ultimate gastronomic experience and sourcing and fidelity to ingredients and foraging and stylistic intention. All of which often boils down to the receipt of a succession of driblets of food of the restaurant's choosing in whatever order it is most convenient for them to serve it, and sometimes even cooking little bits of it yourself: a real night out.

That the form of the crockery will be utterly bizarre is a given – as is the fact that the menu will invariably commence with a 'mission statement', brimming with piety and quite hilarious bombasticism. Make no mistake: concepts are a blight, and thoroughly to be avoided. And the same goes for every variation of a 'themed evening', be it allied to anything at all, from 1970s Disco to the Pride of Scotland. Nor do I need to tell you that any dinner holding out to you the promise of 'an unforgettable evening stepping back into the richness of our heritage' – this very horribly involving 'fine fayre', trestle tables, mead and serving wenches – should be given as wide a berth as is humanly possible.

See also: FASHION, MENUS, SERVICE

CONDIMENTS

'Cruets' have long been no more than the butt of an old joke: the dubious mark of distinction on a table for one in a miserable boarding house with shakers of industrial salt and white pepper and a tiny bowl of Colman's English (this discoloured and crusting over, the dinky little spoon stubbornly immutable since before the war) alongside a defiantly sticky bottle of HP. These days we expect grinders of rock or sea salt and black peppercorns – the latter preferably not leeringly proffered in the form of a three-foot phallus by the sort of Italian waiter to whom you would not care to entrust your wife or daughter (nor even your grandmother, let's face it).

It is rather foolish to reach automatically for the salt or pepper mill and set to twisting away at them before one has actually tasted the food: it should need nothing more, if the chef knows his business – though mercifully, the days of the prima-donna and close-to-deranged star chefs who would evict a diner for so much as requesting salt are now long behind us, the arch offenders now all multimillion-aire television faces and marketeers for stock cubes. Heinz ketchup should always be available for burgers (*pace* the plastic squeezy tomato), no matter what other relishes are on offer, as should be a variety of mustards, including French's and Dijon. If you are in a fast-food joint, all the condiments will come in little squishy sachets. And if you are in a fast-food joint, this is no less than you deserve.

See also: BURGERS, FAST FOOD, SERVICE, STAR CHEFS

CONVERSATION

The ideal meal in a restaurant comprises just everything, to perfection: food, wine, atmosphere, company, comfort, service, decor ... oh, the lot. But for some people, one or other element will be far more important than all the others. To foodies, well, it's obvious really: the grub is all, and while they might well prefer to eat it in a fantastically beautiful room, some dark and fetid shack will do them quite as well. Wine buffs plan the meal around the wonders of the list, and trendies will be delighted simply to be sitting in the hot new place. But conversation looms large on the list: for some, just getting together is the point of the whole thing, the food no more than a sideline – almost an excuse for meeting. And so if a really good chat is central to your meal – maybe in order to catch up with an old chum, close a deal or romantically impress the hitherto unimpressible – then you really must be sure to be in a place where a conversation is even possible. So: you don't want to be in a vast, hard-floored, high-ceilinged and consequently very horribly clattery sort of a place; you don't want to be somewhere that packs in the tables so very tightly that the only conversations you are aware of are those to either side of you; you don't want to be seated in a connecting passageway where waiters will constantly be passing – and nor near the entrance door, the kitchen door or the door to the loos: all are very distracting. And, most important of all, you most certainly don't want to be anywhere at all that is playing – usually for the benefit of the staff – the sort of music at the sort of level that reduces you to wincing, bellowing and craning an ear merely in order to hear and be heard: very soon, you will weary of even the effort to converse – and that, really, is the end of that. All very obvious, I suppose; but if you really do want to have that conversation ... just bear these points in mind, that's all I'm saying. *Can you hear me?* Oh good: well, that's all I'm saying.

See also: ATMOSPHERE, BUSINESS LUNCH, BUZZ, DECOR, MUSIC, ROMANCE, SERVICE, TABLES

CORDON BLEU

Or Le Cordon Bleu, if we're being exact. The famous school of cuisine was founded in France in the late nineteenth century, but the phrase (meaning simply 'blue ribbon', for excellence) remained a fairly well-kept secret amongst the culinary elite until the 1960s – whereupon in Britain cookbooks, recipe cards, snobbery and a general incomprehension rather quickly took over. When told that a meal was cordon bleu, the average rosbif might easily have displayed his utter mystification by tentatively responding, 'Gordon who …?' Better restaurants of the time were keen to be seen to be doing things the right way, the proper way, the old way (with scrupulous attention paid to every division, particular respect given to the patissier), and the British middle class, being the British middle class, sought to emulate that. A course in cordon bleu cookery became one very classy possibility for a daughter (though almost never a son) of the wealthy with time on her hands, no rich fiancé yet, nor particularly fiery or even evident ambition (and always assuming that a Lucy Clayton course in deportment or a Swiss finishing school held no appeal). The phrase 'cordon bleu' did become somewhat diminished as a result of all this, but the real thing is still very vibrant, with scores of highly respected schools all over the world. You are unlikely these days to encounter the term in any other context, though, and certainly not in a restaurant.

See also: FINE DINING, FRENCH

CORPORATE ENTERTAINING

In the light of the behaviour early in the twenty-first century of certain banks and other institutions that add so irrepressibly to the gaiety of all our lives, cosmetic cutbacks were made in the way of corporate entertaining – not because the fat-cat hosts could no longer afford such extremely lavish junkets (it's only taxpayers' money, after all), but because they deemed that, in the 'current climate', it might, just might, 'look bad'. Apparently imagining, therefore, that it actually could look any worse. Oh well.

But you can't keep a good freebie down … and, once again, there is a lot of it about: the good times continue to roll. Lunches at the most prestigious sporting events, very largely – Windsor polo, Lord's Test matches, Wimbledon, Formula One and all the rest of them. International cuisine is the order of the day, anything unthreatening and easily digested that is instantly recognized to be extremely expensive: lobster, chateaubriand, caviar … all aboard the gravy train. Food is there for cachet only – and to help absorb the staggering amounts of drink (which also, but of course, must be instantly recognized to be extremely expensive: Cristal, preferably in magnums, old malt whiskies and so on and so on).

Should you be invited to such an event, all you really need to know is that although the odd nibble is permissible, no one should be seen seriously to eat – and certainly you mustn't be caught dead actually watching the sport, oh God no (and never mind that you're in the very best seats, which the true aficionados had not the slightest hope in hell of obtaining). It's just about drinking, wearing the correct clothes (dark and costly if male, brightly coloured and tear-makingly costly if female), drinking, networking, drinking, and basking in the truth that now and at last you are finally rich enough to be given things free.

See also: BUSINESS LUNCH, CHARITY DINNERS, DRINKING

COURSES

Not as in cookery courses, but as in the succession of plates that are served to you in a restaurant. The rise of the brasserie and gastropub has rather put paid to the necessity of the conventional three-course meal, though naturally this is always available. The trad three courses are in fact a severe contraction of the feasts of old where, following the soup, fish would be de rigueur, and then poultry – all before you got around to the meat course proper. These days, it is perfectly acceptable to have just the one course, although when dining in company a question of etiquette will tentatively poke its potentially embarrassing head above the ramparts. On the whole, it really is best simply to assume that everyone will be having an hors d'oeuvre – because if you say, 'Are you starting …?' another party is likely to say, 'I will if you are …' And the same can happen with pudding, of course. So there is confusion, and instant social malaise: does that mean he wants a starter but if I don't order a starter he will forego a starter and then he won't have a starter and he wants one? Or is he saying that he really doesn't want the bother of a starter but is willing at a pinch to plough through one in order to keep me company if I order one? Ladies who lunch have deftly circumvented the problem by ordering two starters – one of them in place of a fully fledged main – this having the added built-in bonus of making them appear virtuous, discreet in their appetites, and therefore skinny.

The golden rule is always, of course, that everyone should have exactly what they want to eat – no more, no less. So when dining with people whose inclinations are unfamiliar to you, it's as well to establish ground rules. In a place serving primarily burgers, a starter would be unusual … whereas in a more formal place, it would be generally expected. In a tapas bar or somewhere selling small plates, the whole business of courses is neatly sidestepped – as it can be in a Chinese, say. At the opposing end, there is of course the 'tasting menu': this can prove to be a perfectly endless succession of teeny-weeny courses … so do be prepared.

See also: **ETIQUETTE, GASTROPUBS, GUESTS, HOSTS, LADIES WHO LUNCH, MENUS**

DECOR

The decor of a restaurant is its clothes, which sometimes will have been extremely expensively acquired, or else maybe simply scavenged from a skip: but here is its self-perceived image, how it chooses to dress before presenting itself to the world. And – as with clothes – some profess not to care one whit about such surface frippery … while to others, such concerns form the epicentre of their being: a formal religion that is not just merely dutifully observed, but pursued with all the mad-eyed zeal of the recently enlightened.

Ah, but it all used to be so very simple in the old days: a pub was pubby, a local cafe or pasta place was basic, inoffensive and functional … though if a restaurant was aspiring to be noticed and taken seriously, it simply had to look the part – and that meant 'grand': five-star hotel grand, stately home grand. So: towering Corinthian columns, glossy marble, gleaming mirrors and heavily swagged curtains and pelmets, gold leaf in abundance, silk-lined little lampshades, and more than enough glittering silver to render you blind. Many such places still exist, of course – usually within the great hotels – and the best of them are simply glorious and unbeatable (in terms of decor, at least: the food, though always good, never quite seems to measure up to the opulence of its surroundings; maybe it is merely bashful, cowering beneath its silver domes). Flower arrangements in such places as these tend to be deliberately imposing and centrally placed, a vast profusion of expensive fabulousness in usually a very grand urn and easily as fine as a gold medal-winning exhibit at the Chelsea Flower Show, with just a nod towards the displays at the funeral of a particularly vicious and mad East End gangster, who loved his old mum and hated everybody else. The more modern and chic places will go for just the heads of something like lilies at the base of an enormous goldfish bowl, set off by a handful of polished black pebbles (it's art – don't fight it), while simpler restaurants will content themselves with a modest spray or single bloom in a bud vase on the table. Which frequently will be dead. Clusters of wild and foraged greenery are increasingly trendy, though in a vegetarian restaurant these could easily turn out to be your very pricey main.

But now there are all sorts of smart – some so very un-smart as to be smart beyond belief. There is the deliberately blousy *fin de siècle* glamour of the top-flight brasserie and the stark contrast of clean modernity that is the brand of the younger, fashionable, go-ahead chef proprietor (this often to involve iconic furniture and lighting intended to be tacitly acknowledged by the sort of people who utterly delight in tacitly acknowledging such things). Then there is the junk-shop intimacy of bistros and the newer breed of seemingly thrown-together, casual no-booking places and pop-ups ... or the wilful infliction of grunge in the form of salvaged driftwood planking (and the more flaky the paint, the better), stained and galvanized corrugated iron, crumbling exposed brickwork, rusting metal protuberances, reclaimed industrial fittings (upon which often you are seriously expected to sit) and old broadsheet newspapers pressed into service as an ironic nod to napery. Lighting is from the factory floor, and plates and glasses will be of the workhouse variety, in tune with the probably peasant and soup-kitchen food. We also have places that are purposely nothing at all: plain hard floor, white lighting, white paper cloths and napkins (if you're lucky), and a row of hooks on the wall forming the sole adornment (and these places, naturally, are usually very expensive).

All of this, of course, is very much a matter of taste – but from the diner's point of view, you must simply make sure that you are fully aware of the sort of decor you are to be enveloped by, and that you will be comfortable there. If debris as decoration allied with service so very laid back as to be virtually horizontal should offend you ... avoid it. If brutalist surfaces that rebound with clatter and echo appal you ... avoid it. If sipping soup in a ballroom that rivals that at Versailles is likely to cow you into sheepishness ... avoid it. The good news is there is something out there to suit absolutely everyone: you must simply be aware of what is what, that's all.

See also: BISTRO, BRASSERIE, COMFORT, FASHION, GASTROPUBS, SERVICE, STAR CHEFS, TABLES

The dining room at the Ritz – said by many to be the
most beautiful in London. This earnest conference between
all the people who truly matter actually dates from the early 1960s,
but is blissfully timeless: the picture could have been taken
around the *fin de siècle*, or even just a fortnight ago.

DESIGNATED DRIVER

Oh God, what a uniformly miserable thing to be. Why ever did you agree to such a thing? Because it's your turn? Then say that you plan to be ill that evening; tell them you will have died the night before: honour must perforce be laid aside when confronted with the sheer unbridled awfulness of being the designated driver. It's not, of course, the actual driving that's the hardship (although you do sometimes wonder at the thinking behind this entire quite wacky and wholly antisocial concept: what, do taxis not exist where you live, then?), and it isn't even the non-drinking that is the worst of it – though that hardly amounts to 'fun' writ large. No no: the really bad thing is what happens after you have arrived quite jauntily at the restaurant together with your family, together with your mates – checking in the coats, settling down to the menu – cheerfully eschewing the bracing aperitif (not really much of a sacrifice) … and then, as the hours creep by so very horribly slowly, being forced to observe at too close quarters, and thoroughly dumbstruck, just how unbelievably boring, rude, witless, loud, unfunny and frankly dipsomaniacal these people can be – they whom you thought you knew so very well, and among whose jolly company … is usually yourself. It's a sobering thought.

See also: APERITIF, BAR, DRINKING, LIQUID LUNCH

DINNER

Dinner and lunch are rather different creatures. Lunch is taken at a time of day when one is relatively fresh – hence the popularity of business lunches. A business dinner, on the other hand, is more of a self-congratulatory sprawl: the work is over, the deal is done and now we can all get gloriously and expensively blotto because all we have to do afterwards is sleep. While lunch tends quite naturally to begin to break up at a certain hour – with everyone in theory expected to pack into their day just a little bit more – at dinner there is a tacit invitation to linger. A romantic lunch is generally exploratory; a dinner would be more to set the seal upon the thing (and there are candles, which always help).

The other factor people ought to bear in mind is that it will cost more – not in a brasserie, where pricing is constant, but certainly in a fine-dining establishment. And by way of a postscript: it would be as well – if you are either inviting or invited to Dinner, Heston Blumenthal's excellent restaurant in Knightsbridge – to be quite sure exactly what time of day the meal is to occur.

See also: BARGAIN LUNCH, BUSINESS LUNCH, LUNCH, ROMANCE

DOORMEN

Apart from on the steps of the five-star hotels, a doorman these days is very much a rarity. There was a time when even a humble curry house would have shivering on the pavement a resting actor, generally blacked up and tricked out like a rajah – but these days all you might very occasionally glimpse is an unhappy bloke in an ill-fitting topper who, while touching the brim of his hat, often actually omits to perform the opening of the door (and so you do wonder). There is one glowing exception to all this: Sean. Sean has been the doorman at so many top-class London restaurants – and when he moves on, he often seems to attract the diners like a magnet. He knows all the glittering celebs and is something of a star in his own right, while always genial and professional (a fair deal of diplomacy often being required).

It is not mandatory to tip a doorman for opening the door (for if ever there was a job description, this is it), but if he obtains a taxi for you – and particularly if he whistles it up seemingly from nowhere in the teeth of a bitter night – then you really ought to dip into your pocket. Something nominal is all that is required … except, possibly, in the case of Sean, who probably every night is escorted home by Securicor.

See also: FINE DINING, HOTELS, SERVICE

DRINKING

And by drinking, I do mean drinking. Not, for the sake of politesse, being persuaded to have just the one glass of wine with your meal – no no no – but getting seriously stuck into the stuff. So we are talking all lads together, or else the raucous cackle of a hen party, because mixed company does generally tend to be marginally more sensible. Food will usually only get in the way – although the blokes will happily attack a steak, while the ladies (who are likely to be knocking back unseemly quantities of dry white wine made from whatever grape is currently deemed to be the most fashionable) will be pleased by the sight of a prawn or so, or even maybe a Dover sole.

You can tell when drink, not food, is the order of the day: a general reluctance to leave the bar in the first place, and an agitated eagerness to get right back to it. Also much braying laughter at things that are truly not even remotely funny. Some of the older generation will cleave to many-gins-before-the-meal and many-brandies-after-the-meal ... but the real truth is that epic boozing at mealtimes is really not that common any more. People are frightened of getting the sack; people are frightened by the prices. And, of course, if you were to stray from the tolerance of Great Britain and behave like this in America, you would put yourself at risk of being arrested by the 'drink police', who now are in danger of outnumbering even the 'smoking police' – smug and self-appointed vigilantes to a man and woman, with all the zeal of a tyrant. And while the easy process of becoming drunk will always be pleasurable and seductive, actual drunkenness in a public place can never be acceptable: you will hate yourself in the morning, and you may not be alone.

See also: APERITIF, BAR, CORPORATE ENTERTAINING, DESIGNATED DRIVER, LADIES WHO LUNCH, LIQUID LUNCH, PEOPLE, SMOKING, WINE LIST

DUMPS

You can tell if it's a dump from the outside: there's no need at all to go in. It's got lacy cafe curtains hung from a pole – and they're decidedly grimy, maybe even torn. There is a faded and yellow review of the place sellotaped to the inside of the door; it is from a journal you have never heard of and dates from the twentieth century. The paintwork is flaking. Of the three light pendants in the window, one is working. Don't go in. But you are curious, aren't you? You think you shouldn't judge a book by its cover. So you do go in, and what do you see? You see a room that used to be white and is lit like an underground car park. You see someone scowling at you – who then walks the length of the understandably empty restaurant and sternly asks you whether you've booked. The tables are bare wood. And sticky. The menus are laminated. And sticky. There is an indefinable odour, increasingly pervasive, which you eventually identify as being very old oil. The mismatched furniture has been salvaged from a post-war borstal. On the tables are guttered tea lights in jam jars, and a single dead flower. There is a row of dusty, empty wine bottles on a shelf, along with a pair of castanets. And on the tannoy is 1970s disco. The place in which you are standing is a dump. Do I have to tell you to leave immediately? Do you really want to order food from that kitchen, whose greasy and gappy tile grouting may just be glimpsed beyond the flyblown plastic strip curtain? Do you wish to address any further the scowling individual who failed to welcome you? Can you even *contemplate* the state of the loos …? The answer to all of these questions is a thundering 'no'. This is a dump: leave immediately (and it's your fault for going in in the first place – I told you not to).

See also: **DECOR, FRONT OF HOUSE, INEDIBILIA, LOOS, MENUS**

ETIQUETTE

As ever, something of a minefield to the uninitiated – limitless, too, although a great deal of this rather tricky business is covered by other sections in the book (please see the names of the relevant entries at the foot of this piece). All these should take care of the essential etiquette between diners and staff; hosts, guests and fellow diners are something else. Initially, it is as well that all parties are aware of the style of the restaurant – its degree of formality, or else the reverse – and attempt to dress accordingly (though these days, to be honest, exactly what that might mean is frankly anybody's guess). Now, one assumes that no advice is necessary as to the layout of the cutlery and glasses (it is strange that this ever should have caused confusion, as the rule is simplicity itself: start from the outside, and work your way in – always assuming, of course, that the table has been properly set in the first place). Some tables will supply toothpicks in a dinky little silver vase: do not even think of using one. Should an interdental fragment of spinach be proving particularly vexing, attend to it in the lavatory, if you really have to, but never in public. A lady should not overdo the scent: it plays havoc with the subtlety of sauces, and particularly any decent wine.

And talking of ladies … does the gentleman stand when the lady arrives? I think yes – but if you are stuck on the inner banquette, it can become a bit of a performance, and despite your best efforts you do tend for all your trouble to end up looking like Quasimodo. But the banquette, if such is the set-up, should generally anyway be the province of the lady: the rule is, she gets the best view of the room, while you are more than content with feasting upon her unnatural beauty, and the wall behind. And if you are the host, this can be an absolute pain, quite frankly – because while she can see clearly the movements of the waiters, you have to crane around and get a crick in your back every time you wish to summon one. Should the female be the host, however, it is up to her where she chooses to sit; and both you and the sommelier should know that it is she who will be dealing with the wine list, and attending to the tasting (unless she invites you to step in – but don't, for God's sake, offer). All this, of course, assumes a fairly formal relationship between the two of you: if you dine out all the time, you will have your own routine, and will easily fall into it.

If you are a guest, and not great chums with your host, going for the set lunch is always polite – though on the other hand it is up to the host to make clear that you must order whatever you want from any part of the menu (and, if in turn you are extended such largesse, it is bad form to go for the very most expensive dish, and particularly so if you are one of these ungrateful blighters who simply toy with the thing). One further point of etiquette is whether or not you should start without the other party. By this I do not mean that you arrive, order your food and commence to scoff – no, of course not. But is it okay to break bread before anyone else is at table? Should you order a stiffener, and down it? Well, it all depends upon how well you know everyone. If the other person is paying, you should wait until he or she arrives, whereupon drinks can (and should) be ordered. Off your own bat, a jug of water is permissible, of course – although not a pricey bottle of the fizzy stuff (and especially if the other person turns out to prefer the untroubled variety). Whether you should start to eat your main course immediately it arrives on the table (don't want it getting cold!) will not, in a well-run place, ever be a dilemma: all main courses should arrive at precisely the same moment.

If the meal is something of a celebration, then consideration is due to the neighbouring tables: they do not want to hear your speech, nor the constant joyous clinking together of glasses – and certainly not the yapping of your children or, God forbid, the screaming of babies. If this is the nature of the do, you would be better off in a private room, or else somewhere truly raucous and informal. Nor will other diners thank you for being struck instantly blind as the house dims the lights as your blasted birthday cake is trolleyed in.

On another tack – if a man and woman are romantically involved, they simply must keep it clean: no visible hanky-panky … and, come to think of it, none of the concealed sort, either.

Table-hopping is a concern. It is quite all right to wave to people you know – even to stop for a word with them (a word, mind) on your way in or out. But you simply cannot leave your fellow diner stranded alone as you gallivant about the place, glad-handing everyone in sight. Similarly with the smoking thing: you really ought to wait until the end of the meal until you nip out for that gasper, even if the need for it has reduced you to the practically subhuman. If you've got it really bad, apply a nicotine patch beforehand (but don't chew gum). And do I really have to say that mobiles are a no-no …? Now, I know we are inured to seeing two people at table, each of them tapping and swiping away at their phones – taking calls, Instagramming, tweeting (quite possibly each other) and even photographing their plates … but you know in your heart that it's wrong. These people are objects of pity and, increasingly, open derision or anger. So: unless you both are professionals with a ludicrously inflated sense of your own fascination and indispensability, these devices must be turned off. And not laid on the table. And not consulted. Even furtively.

See also: APERITIF, BILL, BOOKING, BUSINESS LUNCH, CELEBRATIONS, CHILDREN, CLUBS, COMPLAINING, EXCUSE FINGERS, FAMILY MEALS, GOING DUTCH, GUESTS, JACKET REQUIRED, ROMANCE, SMOKING, TIPPING, WINE LIST

EXCUSE FINGERS

A branch of etiquette, really – but warranting a separate entry because these days the ruling isn't quite so simple. It used to be that the only foods it was permissible to convey to one's eager mouth by way of the naked fingers were sandwiches, biscuits and cake: so only when taking tea, really. To this modest tally had to be added asparagus and artichoke: the latter fairly obviously, as there is no other sane way to peel away the leaves, but asparagus needs a little qualification. If we are talking about English new-season spears served as simply as they should be (with melted butter, or the rather more yummy hollandaise), then it is indeed correct to pick up each of them by the stump, dip and consume: eat as far down as is pleasant to do so – you don't want to be sucking at a stringy bit. This also works very well with dipping into a boiled egg, preferably duck. But if the asparagus is part of a larger ensemble – salad, say, or grilled with shaved parmesan, perhaps within a sauce or garnish – then clearly you are not required to go through the whole sticky business of picking out each spear with your fingers, but must simply charge in with knife and fork in the usual way.

Then there is the burger. If it is the fully Monty – bun, loaded with everything and squirted with this and that – then most certainly we have before us a hearty two-handed job, no question: to cut it up appears prissy, and destroys the thing. And it is also quite okay to pick up chips as well – and this is true in other contexts, too: if ever they are served (frites, generally) in a little bucket or paper-lined cone. Such as celery sticks and fruit are also finger jobs – though the fruit ought first to be cut or broken into bite-size pieces. Cheese should be applied to bread or biscuit, not gobbled direct. And bread ought always to be broken (not cut) into pieces that can be popped into the mouth whole, and never gnawed at. A postscript on bread: dunking and mopping should really be confined to the company of one's understanding nearest and dearest, and preferably behind closed doors (unless, of course, we are talking about the garlicky sauce that comes with escargots or the creamy wine sauce that accompanies moules marinière, in both of which cases it would take a saint or an ascetic to resist).

The purpose of the ghastly phrase 'excuse fingers' is to request the pardon of the company for having picked up something edible and plonked it down in front of someone else, expecting them then to eat it: no such pardon should be granted, because this is never acceptable unless you are dealing with four-year-olds who have yet to assimilate the apparently boundless extent of your profound ill manners, and know not yet any subtler method of expressing their displeasure than to throw the food back in your face. Lovers will delight in feeding each other with their fingers: it is not just polite but a good deal less nauseating simply to avert one's eyes.

See also: **BREAD AND BUTTER, BURGERS, CHEESE, CHILDREN, ETIQUETTE, ROMANCE, VALENTINE'S DAY**

FAMILY MEALS

Are best taken at home. But if you do seek to venture out, make sure that the mutual love and irresistible foibles that burgeon within your own family are not allowed to spill over on to other tables, where they might just be less well received. A Sunday roast in a gastropub is a reasonable bet: you are quite likely to be surrounded by other families in a similar situation, and a general sort of hugger-mugger and punch-drunk tolerance ought to see you through (provided that your babies aren't just too appalling). There are certain inevitable differences between a family lunch at home and one taken in a restaurant – so do be prepared for the truth that one young child will on principle detest absolutely every single thing on the menu, an older boy will have one too many lagers, father will (yet once more) be horrified by the bill, while gran will find herself at a total loss as to why chicken these days just does not taste of anything at all.

See also: CELEBRATIONS, CHILDREN, ETIQUETTE, GASTROPUBS, SUNDAY ROAST

FASHION

While the nuance and detail of all things fashionable will, by definition, ever be changing, there exist at the very core of this extremely glittery and slippery concept several truths of varying magnitude … though when it comes to restaurants, the cardinal of these is as follows: the most fashionable restaurant of all is the one at which you have no hope whatsoever of securing a table. That's a given – and it's also just the way people want it, really. Think about it: if the lusting would-be punter reads and is told repeatedly that this new and wondrous place is simply the coolest of cool and everyone who is anyone has been spotted there (such frenzied reports sometimes even squeezing in a mention of the food, though this is by no means mandatory), then said lusting would-be punter will actually be rather crushed if his initial request for a booking is met with a breezy, 'Yeah sure, man – no problem, dude!' That which was so easily come by will instantly be diminished and so very much less desirable (manufacturers of top-end handbags and shoes who invent a 'waiting list' having tumbled to the value in all of this cod psychology decades ago). So even if there are tables to be had, the word is put out that they absolutely do not exist. And should you be some intrepid optimist who rocks right up to the restaurant's door unannounced and is amazed to be allowed to sail straight in, they can cover their blushes with the truth that certain tables are always held back in case the odd passing monarch or megastar should care to drop in. And so, as on this particular night in question none such has showed his face … you're in!

But fashionistas are – quite apart from rabid – notoriously fickle. Soon, another hotspot will come to dazzle their horizon … and here looms the moment that the hitherto fashionable restaurant has long been dreading. For to become instantly fashionable is actually not that difficult – wildly, even cripplingly expensive, but not that difficult. You simply have to secure an imposing building at the centre of just everything, and preferably one that was once something else entirely (bank, car showroom, church, factory, museum, mortuary), then get the late David Collins to do the interior and a Michelin-starred chef in the kitchen (nominally, at least). And if the entrepreneur behind the whole caper should be called Jeremy King, Chris Corbin or Richard Caring, then this is seen to be no bad thing. But once you are at the top … the only way is down, no? Well it ain't necessarily so: the trick is in maintaining your cool and street cred along with a solid core of loyal return customers (the holy grail) once the baying hordes of neophiliacs have collectively and raucously hit upon the next big thing. Few, very few ever manage to do this – and those that do manage it come to transcend fashion altogether: decades on, they bask in the heaven of being in big demand and classy, but no longer quite stupidly hot. In London, one thinks of the Ivy (still, yes – although the

Club at the Ivy, for private members, has rather muted its thunder), Le Caprice, J. Sheekey, the Wolseley, Le Gavroche … and, of course, a good few more. While among those that were looking invincible for quite some time but now have rather fallen by the wayside are Langan's Brasserie and Quaglino's. Fashion can be the most duplicitous mistress of all.

Occasionally, a place will become instantly fashionable by word of mouth because it has on its side practically nothing at all: small, workaday and even temporary premises somewhere defiantly obscure, just two people manning the kitchen … But sometimes a spark is lit, and it can truly travel like wildfire: viral, they call it. Keeping the flame alive, however – that is quite another thing. The chief lure of the fashionable restaurant is, of course, the conferral upon the insecure of the ability to tell anyone at all that they have actually dined there and are therefore, by association, wildly fashionable themselves. This, naturally, is all very silly – but fashion is really, isn't it? That, and extremely contagious … though still a lot of fun, if you don't let it get to you.

See also: BOOKING, DECOR, FINE DINING, POP-UPS, STAR CHEFS

FAST FOOD

This need no longer be synonymous with 'junk food' – although for the millions of diehard fans of such totally dire and dangerous fare, it of course still can. For there are many tens of thousands of 'eateries' that will nightly glow like fireflies, all of them catering to the drunk, the lonely, the impoverished, the dispossessed and the frequently deranged: it continues unabated, this tonnage of late-night kebabs, burgers and fried chicken (which never really was that finger-lickin' good; you'd be better off eating your fingers). So, if such is your taste, you'll be fine. For now. Until it all catches up with you.

The famous global chains, of course – most obviously McDonald's, KFC and the rest of them – are very conscious indeed of their public image and reputation, constantly endeavouring to up the apparent 'health' quotient (most often by means of a lettuce leaf).

As a consequence, the actual food in such places is more or less okay (relatively speaking, you understand), while hygiene may generally be depended upon. There are many other chains too now that are not quite as fast as fast – Nando's, say, or Pizza Express – where a degree more comfort is afforded, the food just that little bit better (and, but naturally, that little bit more expensive). But quite recently, a brand-new phenomenon has loomed and blossomed: the serving of very good grub indeed (and not cheap) in pretty much a fast-food environment, the accent very much upon the makeshift, if not ramshackle – most often a superior burger, or spot-on spit-roast chicken. Even in these newly fashionable joints, you are hardly encouraged to linger (either the 'music' or the 'chair' will get to you before too long), but if you are genuinely in a hurry, hungry and even reasonably choosy, you could do worse. Much (see above).

See also: BURGERS, CHAINS, DECOR, FASHION

FINE DINING

It is a phrase that has never sat too happily upon the tongue, recalling on the one hand all those vainglorious superlatives etched into the frosted glass of very run-of-the-mill pubs – 'Best cask ales, fine wines and spirits' (and you knew it was only going to be Double Diamond, Hirondelle and bog-standard Scotch) – and, on the other, the faintest whiff of Hyacinth Bucket. Because it really is so very tempting to pronounce it 'Fane Daning' (this in no way invoking Denmark, by the way, home to what until recently we were rather jokily yet repeatedly informed was 'the best restaurant in the world'). The important thing, though, is to understand just what the term 'fine dining' is generally taken to mean: that the restaurant will almost certainly be in possession of at least one Michelin star, and that the service will be traditional and (with luck) impeccable – as will the decor, the table settings, the level of comfort and the quality of the stemware and napery.

The food, of course, should be first class, and will tend to be French – though often these days with a 'twist' (although twists are best avoided: keep it straight) – while the presentation is absolutely crucial to the whole shebang. It is a given that plates will be very much larger than the food upon them (larger, indeed, than the wheels on your car), and that this food will be – quite literally – as pretty as a picture, much attention having been bestowed upon colour, arrangement, balance and style. Fashions come and go, of course. One year it will be froth or thin pastry curlicues, the next year mousse or a zigzag of coulis (oddly enduring, this one). A rickety tower of food – exactingly constructed with a steady hand and bated breath in the kitchen, such artistic dedication necessitating its instant deconstruction by the diner – will give way to each component arranged around the rim. But the constant is this: it must please the eye, and make you want to eat it.

Quite who decided that this food has to be scattered, built up and nudged around in such a way is moot, but certainly *MasterChef* has a great deal to answer for in propagating the continued compulsion. At its best, fine dining is just that: the best you will encounter, and one of the most heavenly experiences on this earth. The pressure on such establishments is immense (and particularly if they are jockeying for an extra star, and in every diner see lurking a potentially malign food inspector), because any single element that elsewhere might easily go unnoticed – a forgetful waiter, a slight delay, a less-than-sparkling glass – can annihilate the entire experience. And if not for you, then certainly for the dedicated and monomaniacal chef/proprietor: because if, when he has just finished off his own dinner of four espressos and half a dozen cigarettes, he is informed that you are just very slightly upset with the consistency of a sauce, maybe, or the absence of a spoon, he will generally have no recourse but to summarily hang himself.

See also: BARGAIN LUNCH, FASHION, FRENCH, PRESENTATION, RESTAURANT GUIDES, STAR CHEFS, TWISTS

FISH

There have always been fish restaurants … and also fish-and-chip shops. The latter used to be so utterly ubiquitous (and who can forget that wonder without equal? Battered cod and Sarson's-drenched soggy chips late at night in the cold when you are starving?), but now have been much supplanted by fetid clusters of kebab shops, burger bars and fried-chicken joints. But the ones that remain are much treasured – those, at least, that locally have gained a fine reputation. They have upped their game for the increasingly discerning punter, and it sure as hell is paying off.

A curious shifting and blending of the classes and their tastes is more discernible in fish restaurants than in any other outpost of the dining empire. While such excellent specialists as J. Sheekey or Scott's continue to offer the best grilled Dover sole, lobster, turbot, caviar, oysters and all the other top-end and mouth-slavering stuff, so there has slowly occurred a visible democratization in their menus with the appearance of what once was seen to be peasant food: fish pie, fishcakes … and 'beer-battered haddock fillet with fried potatoes', or, put more simply, fish and chips (and that is what you ought to call it when you order – to be so wilfully déclassé always gives both diner and waiter a silly little thrill). The fish pies and fishcakes are generally excellent because the best ingredients are always to hand, and very often become the favourite dishes of all – and this has nothing to do with cost. Things are different down at the chippy, too: while still they sell best the classics (cod, plaice and haddock, although increasingly such as whiting and pollock as well), you will now quite regularly see salmon or sole on the menu. An abiding favourite is scampi – which, interestingly, is one of the things that you will very rarely see offered in a superior restaurant: langoustes and king prawns are fine and dandy, but cover them in breadcrumbs and it would appear that they become instantly rather common.

It is wise to confine your fish consumption solely (ho ho) to fish restaurants: their supplies are of a superior quality, always fresh and constant – and, contrary to myth, this does include Mondays, if the place is any good. But before booking, do for God's sake always ensure that your dining companion doesn't have an aversion or, worse, an allergy. Such plaices (ho ho) always sell the odd meat meal as well, of course – usually steak, to be on the safe side – and one rumour I have persistently heard is that this can in fact be an excellent choice because the chefs are so damn sick of the sight and smell of fish that they take especial care with your sirloin, and cook it with both love and care.

A comparatively recent but ongoing battle that the fish restaurants are forced constantly to wage concerns the shifting uncertainty as to which fish are 'sustainable' and which are on the endangered list. The worry has filtered through to the paying customer, but it really shouldn't. This truly is the responsibility of the restaurant: if a fish is on the menu, you must assume that all is well, and feel free to order with an unsullied conscience. You might just demur at blue-fin tuna and chips, though.

FOOD POISONING

This is very, very rare in a restaurant (in a good restaurant, anyway). Well of course it is: here is the very last thing on earth that they want – the worst publicity of all. A well-run kitchen is scrubbed clean every night and constantly throughout the day, while ingredients of course will be fresh and suitably stored, knives and surfaces properly segregated (one clear benefit of the Health and Safety police: restaurants are certainly kept on their toes). Even so, it does very occasionally happen – and once quite recently at a three-star Michelin restaurant. Now I shan't go into the symptoms of the illness because they are uniformly disgusting, but a reliable way of knowing whether you have in fact been chowing down on food just chock-full of salmonella or E. coli is by whether your dining companions have been similarly afflicted. If such is the case, then it very much looks as if the restaurant is to blame – and attacks can be mild ... or very much not.

Obviously a complaint must be made, and although it remains up to the restaurant how to proceed by way of apology, compensation and tracing the cause, you should – as with all complaints – make clear what you actually want them to do about it, and this will be determined by the severity of the outbreak. If the entire restaurant has been affected, this will become public and the place will be closed down until the source of bacteria is tracked and eliminated.

There are, however (and this will astound you), unscrupulous people who will invent a case of food poisoning purely in order to receive compensation or a free meal. Unfortunately, many restaurants will immediately cave in to such demands – and particularly chains, where if such a complaint became public, it could be absolutely crippling. In most cases, the restaurants know themselves to be innocent of all charges, but the resultant costs and publicity in fighting the claim just aren't seen to be worth the candle. But this is nothing short of theft and slander on the part of the complainant – appalling behaviour all round, which of course no sane or honest person would even consider.

Some people – for which read 'men' – will, the morning following a particularly heavy dinner, blame their dyspepsia and general malaise on 'something dodgy they ate', while the truth lies rather more in the direction of the quantity and potency of something they drank.

See also: CHAINS, COMPLAINING, HEALTH AND SAFETY

FOOD/WINE

As in: what to order with what. The answer being: whatever you damn well like. But although these days it is fashionable – not to say mandatory – to ostentatiously flout accepted 'rules' of any nature, certain guidelines continue to be common sense. There is nothing to stop you (and to blazes with the raised eyebrows) ordering a fine old claret to accompany your Dover sole … but while both these things are much to be prized, not only will they be unenhanced by each other, but also, in this case, they will actually be harmed. But there are lots of reds that will go admirably with fish, if that is your taste – just beware of a heavy one with a light one, if you see what I mean. Young Bordeaux or Côtes-du-Rhône with salmon or monkfish, say, can be good (depending on the sauce), and Beaujolais goes with loads of varieties. Similarly, you can happily drink champagne or Chablis (and certainly Meursault) throughout a hearty meat meal … although a red might just be better.

Some restaurants are particularly known for the quality, breadth or value of their cellar (and, if you are inordinately fortunate, all three). This attracts oenophiles like midges to a picnicker – and of course they will sensibly start with an intense perusal of the wine list, and eventually work their way to the menu. If the wine selected is truly starry, then the very simplest grilled food is ideal, and with no intrusive sauces – for most often it is not the actual food but the sauces that will mingle badly with the wine. Often – with a posh bargain lunch or a tasting menu – the chef and sommelier will jointly have done the work for you: a suitable choice of wine will be served with each successive course (and it would be boorish and swaggering of you to reject these in favour of others). In summer, when food is lighter and perhaps al fresco, a lot of reds may be chilled, on request: the sturdier Beaujolais, most obviously, but also such as southern Italians – Sangiovese, that sort of thing. Ultimately, you must enjoy what you enjoy, because remember: it's your palate, your meal, and you are paying the bill.

See also: **BARGAIN LUNCH, BYO, OUTDOOR EATING, SAUCES, SOMMELIERS, WINE LIST**

FORAGING

....

While picking wild mushrooms for the cooking pot is an ancient practice (although as a result of it, if you don't know what you're doing, you do tend to die), a relative newcomer to all this sort of self-sufficiency thing goes by the name of 'foraging'. Not as during active service in

There is foraging … and then there is foraging.
Here, we have a pig in quest of something you would actually
want to share: a truffle. At most of what is foraged today, however,
said pig would disdainfully turn up its snout.

a war, when some poor devil was charged with venturing out into a bullet-strafed no-man's-land in order to find such as a pig or even apples or potatoes to keep his fellow soldiers from starvation – no no – but the searching for, oh, I don't know ... all sorts of little unconsidered leafy and twiggy trifles. The most famous and pioneering restaurant to go in for this lark is Noma in Denmark, recently reputed to be the best restaurant in the entire world, if you choose to believe such a thing. So each morning at dawn or earlier, in order to eke out actual food, all the neighbouring byways, banks and bogs are scoured for the kinds of accumulation that traditionally people have, upon arriving home, scraped off the soles of their wellingtons. All fine if you can be bothered and are aware of what you are about, I suppose – but you are not urged to try this at home.

FOREIGN

Abroad is supremely important, because without it the British would be cruelly denied the inexpressible joy of leaving, and coming back home again. But many of us do owe to abroad a particular debt, because it was probably in some or other outpost of it that we first discovered just how food and eating out really could be. Which, admittedly, was often way beyond quite hellish – but when it was good, it tended to be wonderful. What we should by now know about restaurants in foreign parts, however, is that the food, wine and service that seem just perfectly perfect on a shaded terrace, the bougainvillea vibrant against an unbroken Mediterranean sky ... will not at all translate to Wigan or Bayswater, and it is folly to expect it. I have no idea why Wigan and Bayswater have been singled out in so invidious a manner, but they serve to make the point. And, incidentally, it is no longer remotely worthwhile to attempt to take home with you a little piece of paradise by loading up the car with flagons of local wine, olive oil, cheese or whatever, because upon your return you will find that said flagons of local wine now taste as poisonous as petrol, the cheese or whatever will have oozed, and the olive oil – though fine – would have cost you a great deal less in Waitrose.

See also: CHINESE, FRENCH, INDIAN, ITALIAN, SPANISH

FORMAL DINNERS

Formal dinners are different from ordinary dinners in that their primary concern is rarely either food or enjoyment, and hence they are not nearly so good as ordinary dinners, which actually have their priorities right. A formal dinner will entail not just strangers but also black tie (or even white tie, at the very most formal of the formal) and evening dresses, so guests may not always be quite as comfortable as they might have preferred. Often you will have to whisper your name, maybe even spell it, to a toastmaster so that he can boom it out to all and sundry, possibly even correctly – and there has yet to be born the person who could be comfortable with that. There will be a *placement*, and here is the rub: you are compelled out of *politesse* to converse equally and in turn with the person to either side of you, and in addition to those you really can only hope to attempt to talk to the one or two opposite … and so if they turn out to be bores, loudmouths, drunk or messy eaters, you are rather up a gum tree, aren't you?

The food will be designed to cause as little offence as possible, and so, if you are lucky, it will cause you little offence. And then there will be speeches: here are the *raisons d'être* of a formal dinner. Most would agree that the only thing more lowering than the approaching inevitability of a speech is actually having to get up and make one yourself. If this is the order of the day, then unless you are a seasoned professional, you will have been anxiously fingering your notes beneath the table, trying not to drink while desperately needing to, not listening properly or even at all to your dining companions, and almost certainly saying nothing remotely of interest, or even lucidity. The good news about such events, however, is that you don't have to think: you are instructed where to sit, given what you are expected to eat, and told when to leave. And that moment, of course, is the best part of all.

See also: CHARITY DINNERS, PRIZE DINNERS

FRENCH

French cuisine is the finest in the world. And if you hum about that, or should you haw – if in any way you seek absolute reassurance of the fact … well then just ask anyone French. For to a man and woman, they are inordinately proud of their food and wine – and so they damned well should be, for their contribution to the world of gastronomy is truly incalculable. That said, it would be rather nice if they didn't go on about it quite so much, and could bring themselves to be slightly less smug. Because the truth is, you see, that they do not see themselves as contributors to the world of gastronomy so much as the sole creators who own the copyright; they do not simply believe that French restaurants are the best – which is certainly arguable – but that they are the only ones worth bothering with in the whole of the world. And if you gently indicate that, in the view of many, the restaurant scene in London has now eclipsed that of Paris, they will counter by informing you that the only decent restaurants in London employ French chefs; and although that is untrue to the point of lunacy, just you try telling them that.

Similarly, many highly civilized and foodily knowledgeable and experienced French people who find themselves in London will shun anything remotely akin to an English restaurant (and these days there is a very good selection of such establishments) because, to them, the very juxtaposition of the words 'English' and 'food' is hardly more than a very good joke – because just as all Americans know that the English all day are uttering such things as 'I say I say I say gorblimey have a cup of tea righto Jeeves apples and pears splendid God bless the Queen cheerio Mary Poppins', so the French are aware that we live solely on boiled potatoes, steak-and-kidney pie, bacon and eggs and fish and chips. So instead they will either go to a middling brasserie or bistro and pronounce it far less good than their favourite in France, or else ferret out a Michel Roux, a Pierre Koffman or an Alain Ducasse in order to prove their point. Unlike the British, they simply refuse to believe that the times they are a changin' – and that while no one is in any doubt that the best of French is the best there is to be had, there are also a great number of so-called French restaurants that are just about okay, if not actually abysmal and madly overpriced due to their stubborn immutability with regard to ingredients and sauces, and wholly misguided pretensions. One day the French may come to see that cuisines from alternative continents do actually have their place in the universe, as does wine that fails to hail from Bordeaux, Burgundy or Champagne. For even Michelin, that Gallic bible of culinary excellence, is bending to the spirit of the age: there are many starred restaurants now that even a decade ago would not have been considered because the chef, service or decor did not conform to the traditional norm.

French waiters have a reputation for rudeness (as Italian waiters have a reputation for lewdness). In my experience, however, this tends to be true only in tourist hotspots in France, where understandably they are just about sick to bloody death of particularly Americans making no effort whatsoever with their language ('Yeah, uh – can I get a coffee over here, and the tab …?') and then ordering the croque-monsieur because it's the cheapest thing they can find on the menu, before making some or other crummy joke about its name, and then getting into a mess with their unaccustomed euros. In a good restaurant – in France and all over the world – a properly trained French waiter is the best there is: he sees himself quite rightly as an essential part of the dining process and does not (you will hardly need to be told) feel himself to be in any way menial. And the same goes for the sommelier.

See also: **BISTRO, BRASSERIE, FINE DINING, RESTAURANT GUIDES, SERVICE, SOMMELIERS, STAR CHEFS, WINE LIST**

Only the larger and better established restaurants will boast the luxury of a proper 'front of house' – though, in truth, it is not actually a luxury at all, but absolutely fundamental to the clockwork running of the place. He will welcome you – preferably by name, because he will have been mugging up on the bookings (and certainly by name if you are a regular) – and then he will either personally escort you to your table, or whisper its number to someone other, who then will attend to it smoothly. If you have a coat, hat or baggage to leave, that will be taken care of (unless there is a dedicated cloakroom – yet even then, a good front of house will relieve you of the bother of seeing to it yourself). If you are a regular, you will be taken to your usual table; or else, if it is not available (and he will have striven, but occasionally there just has to be an unavoidable clash) something similarly good, the blow perhaps softened by means of a complimentary glass of something. If you are not a regular but have specifically requested a certain table (and this has been agreed by the restaurant at the time of booking), it is the responsibility of the front of house to make sure that you get it.

The front of house's duties are not confined to front of house, though – for his eyes, they have to be everywhere. The best of them develop a very special sense of when all is running smoothly – that wonderful hum of a perfectly run restaurant – or whether there is looming an incipient wrinkle, the merest rustle, even if it is noiseless: they will detect it by means of their unique antennae when a problem is about to arise, and deftly deflect it; and if something actually does go wrong, they will swiftly rectify it, according to your wishes. They are, let's face it, Jeeves with knobs on, and the best known are regularly headhunted by rival establishments (the very best of the best – Robert Holland at the Wolseley, say – remaining loyal).

It hardly needs me to point out that these peerless wonders, comparable with the legendary concierges in the finest hotels, are hardly to be confused with the person who looks up idly from a computer screen and stares at you quite without curiosity as you walk in the door. You say 'Hello', and he says 'Have you booked?' Even worse is the gaggle of sleekly gorgeous women dressed in black who not so much stare as glare as they run down their seemingly endless lists of the honoured with a red japanned talon. Not for nothing has this singularly belligerent tribe been christened the Clipboard Nazis: it is as if they are not so much greeting a paying guest as exercising extreme suspicion as to your motives and credentials. They can on occasion resort to outright aggression in their determination to repel anyone they perceive to be an unwelcome invader – and, even if they have reluctantly come to agree that you do in fact have a booking at this precise hour, will on principle siphon you away to the bar, where at their whim you are expected to stew, and expensively. As soon as you enter a restaurant, you will know what sort of front of house you have got: this will determine whether you want to stay, and certainly whether you have the slightest intention of coming again.

See also: BAR, BOOKING, CLOAKROOM, COMPLAINING, FASHION, REGULAR HAUNTS, SERVICE, TABLES

FUSION

Confusion ... that might be a better word – because it includes the element of 'con' that always somehow lurks here, as a sneaking suspicion. For it's hard enough, many would agree, getting to know your way around a certain sort of established menu without their suddenly conflating them all so that you hardly know which way to turn. It all started with Asian restaurants seeking to cover the waterfront, as it were: all the Chinese regions and divisions on the one menu – this in order to display versatility in the kitchen and offer a diversity of choice in order to appeal to the broadest church. Then a bit of Thai would creep into it ... Vietnamese ... Korean ... good grief. But all of this is still just about okay, because there is, after all, a tangible denominator. But then the fad began to spread: a clearly Western restaurant would be serving defiantly oriental starters, say – which is also okay: you see them on the menu, you order them or you don't. But soon we began to see a Western dish with an oriental sauce or accompaniment ... and then things started to get a bit weird – because let's face it: you only had the word of the conceivably schizophrenic and very possibly dangerously deluded chef that the resultant melange would be anything other than quite utterly disgusting.

The trouble is, 'fusion' has come to be seen to be clever in itself – and in the right hands, of course, there can result a brilliance both creative and surprising (often what a palate is craving), while at its worst ... here is just a question of bunging together a highly unlikely assortment of components garnered from all over the place, crossing your fingers and hoping for the best: what we used to refer to simply as 'buggering things about'. There are all sorts of so-called fusions that now appear to have become mainstream – possibly the oldest, best known and most repulsive of them being that thing they call 'surf 'n' turf': a piece of fish or some prawns nestled up to a hunk of meat. Is that a good idea? Why is that a good idea? And even more recently, in some of the more fashionable joints, steak is being served with a lump of lobster on the top of it. And that isn't, just isn't, a good idea. Is it? No, it isn't. Do-it-yourself fusion is the latest potential nightmare: these all-you-can-eat joints offering not just Chinese, Japanese and Thai, but also Italian, Spanish, Indian, Mexican ... so that some starving halfwit can finally get to taste a chicken tikka masala with a bit of sushi, a chunk of tortilla and a scattering of tacos – topped by maybe just a soupçon of tagliatelle carbonara, for novelty's sake. So, in short: know your restaurant, and trust it wholly. And the same goes for your stomach.

See also: ALL-YOU-CAN-EAT BUFFET, CHINESE, FISH, STEAK, TWISTS, UNUSUAL

GASTROPUBS

Nobody seems terribly to care for this hybrid word 'gastropub', but I suppose it will have to do. First coined, I imagine, simply to differentiate the alluring newness of the beast from the simple old-fashioned corner boozer (which was the origin of practically all of them), where, if hunger came upon you, you might if you were lucky be able to get hold of a packet of smoky bacon crisps, a bag of peanuts ripped from a card depicting a pneumatic and colourful doxy who became progressively nuder as more of the peanuts were sold, conceivably even some sort of a pie of dubious origin, not to say content … and that was just about it. And there was nothing much wrong with that, actually: a pub was a pub. It was meant for drinking beer in – the kinds of real ale, maybe, that people who are seriously into real ale will talk about endlessly while they continue to quaff, and to the complete exclusion of absolutely all else. The pub was also the place where the solitary old geezer could go and sit in his corner on his regular chair with a pint, the racing page and a fag, and he'd be right back there the same time tomorrow, you could set your watch by him. But … there was no money in old geezers like that, as very soon the brewers came to realize. So along came the interior decorators and out went the dartboards, snugs, pickled onions and coagulated carpets (not to say the old geezers, poor devils), and in came blackboard menus, lengthy wine lists where once there had been a choice only of long-ago-opened red vinegar or white, a wood-fired oven and a hotchpotch of mismatched furniture that was a good deal older and more ramshackle than much of the stuff they'd just chucked out.

And now, there is practically no other sort of pub to go to. The old geezer stays at home these days, while he picks the day's losers on the racing page – and at least there he can still smoke a fag and the supermarket beer costs a quarter of what they charge in a gastropub. But he'll miss his corner and his usual chair in that old boozer, which he knows to his pain has long been overrun by trendies and children.

The quality of food, comfort and service in gastropubs varies enormously – and if you know of a good and handy one that you're on the whole pretty pleased with, then you'd be well advised to stick with it. The independent one-offs are generally sound because they just have to be in order to survive in a very crowded marketplace, and of course they will try that little bit harder. That said, some chains do the thing really awfully well, the food actually very impressive, the ambience comfortable, the service friendly, the prices not too alarming … while others treat their customers with an almost wilfully arrogant contempt (and the customers, they bloody well deserve it, if they're foolish enough to keep on going back). There is a lowering and certain sameness about each and every one of them, though – as if the designers had all attended the very same gastropub night school, and cribbed one another's notes. The pews and chapel chairs with the box at the rear for a hymnal (you do have to wonder whether the few remaining churches that haven't yet been converted into either bingo halls or 'luxury loft living' are not these days all rammed full of bar stools, cribbage sets and horseshoe bars replete with pumps). Sticky tables fashioned from Singer-sewing-machine bases and a hunk of driftwood. The reproduction enamel advertising signs, ironic standard lamps from granny's front parlour with fringed and tasselled shades, cutlery and green paper napkins in a bucket on the table, jokey names for the Gents and Ladies. The 'gourmet' take on such old staples as Scotch egg and pork pie, the wines so wittily categorized into Good, Better, Best, the flyers eulogizing their Sunday roasts and with news of a coming barbecue … and then, finally, the bill at the end of it all that makes you go, blimey O'Reilly: for that sort of money, we could have gone to a proper restaurant.

See also: BAR, CHAINS, COMFORT, DECOR, DRINKING, FASHION

GLAMOUR

The Ritz: sometimes, you know, you really ought to be putting it on. When the occasion demands, glamour can be fun – so away with dressing down, slobbing out and coming as you are, the time for bling is now! A formal dinner presents the most obvious possibility for the pushing out of sartorial boats – and dressing for them is usually the only reason women will ever agree to attend such generally grisly functions in the first place. But why not just for the hell of it? A three-piece suit: how long has it been? What about decent cufflinks and that gorgeous and chunky gold watch that you hardly ever wear any more, not really for the reason that it's too expensive to insure it, but actually because you're absolutely terrified of getting mugged? The ladies will need no instruction whatsoever on how to do this thing: it is simply a question of unstopping the dam of glam desire that has perforce been stemmed for just about ever. Do always make sure, though, that the venue lives up to your fabulous presence, and you'll be rewarded: all the fine restaurants and hotels that take inordinate pride and trouble over the perfection of the decor and detail, the tables and the flowers, the lighting and the service, in their breathtakingly beautiful rooms are actually quite delighted when diners pay them the compliment of making a similar effort – and how much better the room looks when filled with glamorous people.

I am reminded of dinners laid on by the glorious British Pullman train – coffee-and-cream livery, magnificent art nouveau and art deco interiors filled with marquetry, Lalique glass, brass and silver – which for some dinners specify black tie, while for others they simply encourage 'dressing up'. All you have to remember is to make sure that everyone in the party is aware of the glamorous intention, and is absolutely up for it: the last thing we want to see is some poor sap in a V-neck, looking appalling and feeling even worse.

So, there we are: once in a while, just let it rip. Go forth and dazzle.

See also: DECOR, ETIQUETTE, FORMAL DINNERS, JACKET REQUIRED, TRAVEL EATING

GOING DUTCH

If there is no prior agreement and tentatively you are feeling your way, then here of course can be a veritable minefield ... or otherwise, simply how a couple or group chooses to go about things. In the old days, it was all so simple (as if you need me to tell you that): there was really never a question of going Dutch – the man paid, and that was that. If we were talking two men, then the senior or host would pay ... with a tacit understanding that upon the next occasion, he would be the guest. Splitting the bill was generally confined to groups of students and workmates, and that convention persists. Bevies of women in particular still seem to be wedded to the idea, and this can make for considerable embarrassment and annoyance – if not to them, then certainly among the surrounding tables – because they do tend to be absolute sticklers over the nitty-gritty: if there are four of them, say, the bill will rarely be split straightforwardly into equal quarters ... 'because you three started with a glass of champagne and I'm pregnant and on the wagon as well you all know and I didn't eat any of the pommes dauphinoise and had the merest spoonful of sorbet so I don't see why I should pay for any of that although I did admittedly order a pot of peppermint infusion and I don't mind chipping in for a bit of the Chardonnay although I didn't actually drink any and I wouldn't actually mind another peppermint infusion as it happens and I didn't consider the service up to much so I'm not particularly keen to be part of whatever percentage charge they've gone and slapped on but apart from all that I'm completely fine with it being divided four ways'. And if another of the party is similarly nitpicking and cheeseparing, the endgame of the meal can very rapidly descend into a quite shrill brawl of accountancy, the table littered with cash, cards and hastily scribbled subtractions and long divisions.

If you lunch or dine regularly with a certain person or group, it is rather more civilized (and certainly quicker) simply to take turns with the bill, no questions asked – though this does not give licence to one of the party to get smashed on fine wine on the occasions when someone else is paying, while piously sticking with tap water when it is their turn. With couples – a man and a woman – things are trickier. When it used to be the unspoken and unbroken convention that a man would always pay for everything (and among the older generation of gentlemen unused to the predominance of high-flying career women, this still will be the rule, as they demonstrably feel uncomfortable with it any other way), obviously it was rude and looked very mean if ever he suggested the splitting of the bill – and a potentially tricky situation could loom if the lady had come unprepared. And if it were she who suggested a division of the cost (as many did, either from a sense of fairness and generosity, or else because they did not wish to feel in any way compromised – this, in turn, often being the man's entire intention), then it was expected that the man would politely decline the kind offer. These days, women are very often in a strong financial position and are quite used to running things their way … but still, on either side we really do not want anything in the way of a power play, do we? Best for one of them to pay the bill outright, and accept graciously the offer of a reciprocal meal another time soon at the expense of the other party (and this offer must be not only voiced, but also executed). Should you be dining with one of your employees, children, someone visibly desperate for a solid meat meal or else a person you are madly desperate to seduce … then of course it is your treat. Obviously.

When dining with a man, a woman can often find that her insistence upon paying the bill or even going Dutch is met with resentment, hostility or the horrified (and horrifying) blush of abject humiliation. This is not the fault of the woman, but simply a demonstration of the lily-livered lack of confidence in the man: he simply must brace himself and take courage (Dutch or otherwise).

See also: BILL, BUSINESS LUNCH, ETIQUETTE, GUESTS, HOSTS, LADIES WHO LUNCH, ROMANCE

GOURMETS AND GOURMANDS

It is surprising to discover just how many people seem to believe that these two words are merely synonymous. A gourmet is, of course, one who is an epicure, a connoisseur of the finest cuisine the world has to offer, while not necessarily possessing the ability to create it. Without the gourmet, haute cuisine would soon look very silly indeed, as there would be no one left to flog it to. Being a gourmet is fine, so long as you do not so much as dream of announcing yourself as such. And please, don't go on about the breadth of your knowledge, and particularly in a restaurant: no one appreciates a show of one-upmanship, so do at all costs try to refrain from explaining in depth how you perceive a certain sauce to be a valiant effort, though 'inaccurate', because no one, believe me, will give a single damn. There are some gourmets, however (actually quite a few, if I'm being honest here), who seem to be totally incapable of talking about anything other than food and wine – and certainly never when they are actually in the act of consuming it (which is usually). Examples: if you tell them you have just got back from a holiday in Spain, they will tell you in return that they personally have always favoured Italy, which puts them in mind of this most wonderful little restaurant in a hard-to-get-to part of the Puglia region that has been there for centuries but isn't for some reason even on the map and there is no actual menu but there I remember eating quite the most unforgettable … blah blah blah. And if you say you have just bought a new car, they will inform you that they no longer bother with driving because you cannot park outside any decent restaurant and nor can you complement your meal with a wonderful vintage once you are settled into your habitual table that the front of house there who is a personal friend always sees to it that you have – and that is especially true of this one particular very fine restaurant in a cul-de-sac in actually quite a rough part of town but if you are in the know and ask for Giovanni they will cook for you a seafood pasta, generally angel hair, that isn't actually on the menu but honestly is quite the most utterly sublime … yadda yadda yadda. These people: they got it bad. Tell them your entire family has just been wiped out by a tornado and they will blithely recall a trip to Fiji where they enjoyed a funeral breakfast that was ambrosial, and second to none.

While a gourmand is a pig.

See also: ETIQUETTE

GREASY SPOONS

There are few more welcoming sights on a cold, wet day when you are absolutely starving beyond all belief than the steamed-up windows of a greasy spoon. And make no mistake, the windows should always be steamed up; if they're not steamed up, something's wrong: don't go in. Called a 'greasy spoon' with affection – maybe because once upon a time the spoon for stirring everybody's tea was chained to the counter – it is rarely the venue of absolute choice, but by God you could do a whole lot worse. They are not nearly so numerous as they used to be because 'working-class areas' are no longer so easily defined (and, according to estate agents, in fact no longer in existence). But still a fair deal of the rough-and-ready high streets in less gentrified areas will have a decent example lurking somewhere. In fact, a few in the East End of London and Westminster have been raised to the level of absolute classics of the genre due to their unaltered facades and interiors (this originally due less to preservation than to indolence), and hence are now visited as if on a pilgrimage by students of design, inverted snobs and assorted moneyed clever Dicks who just thrill to the blissful irony of it all – much to the open loathing and queasy disgust of the salt of the earth who still actually go there simply in order to get filled up cheaply.

For that's what you must want of a greasy spoon – to get filled up. You don't pop in for a croissant and a skinny latte, no no no. What you go in there for is three slices of fried bread, two eggs, two sausages, three rashers of bacon, fried mushrooms, fried kidneys, grilled tomatoes and two rounds of black pudding, all amid a pool of luminous baked beans, as well as – if you're hungry – a plate of chips. All, it goes without saying, with much HP and ketchup. Plus tea. Great thick mugs of builder's tea with five spoons of sugar. And – because the greasy spoon is the perfect place to go to alone (you really don't want to socialize in these places: keep yourself to yourself, that's the ticket) – don't forget to bring along your copy of *The Sun*, folded either to the racing or else to all the bouncy fulsome bounty of Page Three Chantelle from Billericay, licking a cornet. Breakfast, they say, is the most important meal of the day – and you can get it in the greasy spoon any time at all, from dawn till dusk.

See also: BREAKFAST, CAFES, FAST FOOD, SOLO DINING

GUESTS

It is, to a degree, the duty of the guest to conform – though not to the point of failing to enjoy himself (always assuming that the lunch is not some sort of ghastly disguise for a job interview, on which occasions of course the sole intention of the host is to make him suffer). By conform I mean that when invited to a certain restaurant or club at a particular hour, he should not counter-suggest somewhere different slightly earlier or later: he accepts with pleasure, or declines with regret. If there is a set lunch option on the menu, and the host makes it clear that here is his own intended route (which he absolutely shouldn't), then the guest ought really to conform to this as well. If encouraged to explore the carte (as he absolutely should be), then he may feel quite free to let rip.

The guest should neither order nor taste the wine unless invited to do so – and he should applaud his host's selection, unless it is actually corked and undrinkable (though the host should have assured himself that it isn't). It's a tricky one, actually, if the host has okayed a bad wine: in the old days, etiquette would have dictated that the guest simply choke it down, refer to it, if at all, as 'interesting', and defer all nausea and mouth-puckered disgust for later. This just simply shouldn't happen nowadays: dining is all about pleasure, which should never be forgotten – so a gentle remark about the wine being singular, not quite usual, might be in order. This, accompanied by the raising of an eyebrow, ought to be sufficient to alert your host. If it isn't, then he is a palate-dead numbskull, and you shouldn't be with him in the first place.

The guest should not suggest lingering at the end of the meal over another round of coffee and maybe booze, but if this is suggested to him by his host, he is perfectly at liberty to stay, or else excuse himself – at lunch, but less so at dinner. He must also contribute: not financially, of course, but by way of witty and light conversation, and being general good value (though not through having recourse to endless prepared anecdotes, and certainly not – obviously – a string of 'jokes'). The only other thing a good guest simply must remember (apart from dressing appropriately for the venue – up or down) is that upon the next occasion, he will be the host.

See also: **ETIQUETTE, HOSTS, JACKET REQUIRED, MENUS, WINE LIST**

HEALTH AND SAFETY

The very phrase! It's so very lowering, isn't it? Deadly, really. The nanny state has long ago decided that if the civilized diner wishes to observe the time-honoured and traditional delight of enjoying a fine Havana cigar following his dinner ... then in order to do so he must bugger off to some flyblown scrap of dirt designated as an area for the fetid bins – and probably in the rain as well, while gnashed by the fangs of a gale. His own health and safety is not an issue, of course; should he contract pneumonia, well, that's just too bad, but at least everyone else in the vicinity will be rescued from the unutterable hell of 'passive smoking'. Fine – there may or may not be a point to that. But now unwelcome attention has been diverted to the actual food upon one's plate.

By law, no restaurant now is permitted to serve a rare burger (so for how long steak tartare can manage to hold its place on a menu is just anyone's guess). A proper mayonnaise is becoming very hard to come by, because it is strongly suggested that eggs should always be cooked through: most restaurants are more than happy to conform to this stipulation, not for the sake of their customers' constitution, but rather to deflect all possibility of a law suit. Some restaurants will cite this nonsense as a reason why the poached egg in your breakfast or atop the smoked haddock must also be as bouncy as Silly Putty. Unpasteurized cheese? A rarity now, for much the same reason. The delight of a deft head waiter demonstrating his skills at the table with a dazzling silver burner and skillet in order to produce such archaic wonders as steak Diane and crêpes Suzette ... all but vanished. The amount of calories contained in each dish is increasingly sneaking into menus – and soon, alcoholic 'units' will start to appear next to the vintage of a wine. Doubtless alongside a po-faced reminder to always observe several 'alcohol free days' each week. Well I'm all for that, at least: you show me where the free alcohol is, and I'll be there for as many days as you want me, matey.

See also: BURGERS, CHEESE, DRINKING, FOOD POISONING, SERVICE, SMOKING

HOSTS

There are two ways of looking at this little word 'host'. At its most basic, it simply means that you are the person who has instigated the lunch or dinner, and therefore will have proposed both date and venue, with the tacit understanding that you also will be footing the bill. Or else it might be a bit of a do … in which case there is a bit more to it: greeting people on arrival (at the door, if you have booked a private room – otherwise just springing to attention at the table as each successive person clocks in), maybe seeing to a *placement*, and making any necessary introductions. In either case, though, the intention is the same: to make your guests as comfortable as possible (in every sense) and ensure that they have what they want – just fundamental manners, really. This means not inviting two people who are known to be at loggerheads (and particularly, dear God, if they are divorced from each other), making sure that everyone is aware of the dress code, if there is one, and that all 'special requirements' (usually vegetarianism and allergies) have been catered to. Be generous: in no way inhibit your guests' inclinations by saying such things as, 'I'm having the set lunch – it's always reliable', or, 'Will you be wanting a glass of wine with that …?' It doesn't mean, though, that you are there simply as a back-up maître d': it is most important that you have a jolly time as well, and are seen to … but it just must be remembered that your guests come first. *C'est tout.*

See also: **CELEBRATIONS, ETIQUETTE, GUESTS, SPECIAL REQUIREMENTS**

HOTELS

Back in the day, if any sort of even vaguely special lunch or dinner was required, a hotel was the natural choice – largely because (and this was particularly and very painfully true in provincial towns) there simply didn't exist a great deal of choice in the matter, and the better hotels could at least be depended upon to provide some reasonably grand spaces, together with the kind of often very inept and overblown pomp that people unaccustomed to paying through the nose will, along with a large degree of coddling, habitually require (this to soften the blow – as hotels well understand, and hence they are very good at chucking it in by the bagful). These days, however, hotels have to work rather harder for our custom, because now there are just so many really fine stand-alone restaurants that themselves are no strangers to the dazzle of display, flattery and tip-top service. Even residents in hotels will by no means necessarily eat there – and especially in London, where competition in every quarter is simply ferocious. Now hotel food, of course … when it is bad, it tends to be very bad indeed – although that said, there are now a lot of starred hotels that, having wisely assimilated all of the above, have considerably upped their game, hiring big-name chefs and fashionable franchises to transform their fusty dining room into a must-go destination restaurant.

There are unique advantages to hotels: they will almost certainly have a private room, should such be required for a celebration; they have decent and comfortable bars for those all-important pre- and post-prandial tipples; and, of course, they have rooms. Rooms can be very useful indeed if people have travelled from all over the place, and the evening looks like being a long one: how very much more pleasant a prospect is a good night's sleep in a peaceful room following all that grub and booze than the thought of an arduous drive back home in the drizzle and the dark, having not been allowed to drink a bloody thing. And even after lunch … if, along with the food and wine, should either fresh seduction or the rebooting of a slumbering passion be looming large on the menu – well, then a hotel: it's just so very accommodating.

See also: BAR, CELEBRATIONS, DESIGNATED DRIVER, DRINKING, ROMANCE, SERVICE, STAR CHEFS

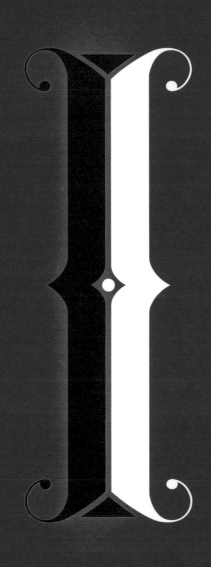

Indian restaurants, we are told, have long been the nation's favourite. Really? Are we absolutely sure about that? I mean, I know that statistics demonstrate that the sales of chicken tikka masala outstrip those of fish and chips and just about everything else, but does that really mean that Indian is Britain's number-one go-to cuisine? Not really. Because although there do exist many superior Indian restaurants, a few of them even passingly fashionable, it is the little local with bedroom wallpaper and Ronsealed plywood fretwork that is king: the destination of choice for those people who frequently are given to expressing the belligerent desire to 'murder a curry', this urge to kill very largely prompted by the growing realization that prior to the gentle and convivial sipping of twelve or so pints of lager in the company of like-minded individuals, with the exception of a bowl of Golden Grahams about twenty-four hours back and a Twix with their tea, they haven't actually eaten within living memory. The local Indian is open … and so in they totter. And apart from the lure of something quick and cheap to blot up the booze, there is the added massive appeal of the macho element. For it is a given that they will plump for the hottest curry on offer: there can simply be no debate about it (and God help anyone in the company wimpish enough to opt for a korma when it's vindaloos all round). And so they seamlessly segue from loud competitive drinking to probably no less noisy competitive eating.

Even the more upmarket Indian restaurants are capitalizing on the phenomenon of these individuals' fathomless and eager stupidity. One such in London – with a renowned star chef – recently introduced a selection of dishes so almost literally mind-blowingly hot that diners were required to sign a disclaimer. Honestly. A disclaimer: so that if, as a result of lunch, you suffer permanent internal injury or even death (they could murder a curry eater), it is no fault of the restaurant. Well yum yum: bring it on (I don't think). One dish contained naga bhut jolokia chillies … which are used by the Indian army in the form of a spray that completely blinds and incapacitates any unfortunate passing marauder. Nice. An alternative dish boasted as its prime ingredient the 'Trinidad Scorpion'. Now, you know Tabasco sauce? Hot, yes? Well, the Trinidad Scorpion is hotter – by a factor of four hundred. And there you have it: one for the real men, eh? The ones who either have left their brain at home on a shelf, or else have long ago allowed it to be fried by chilli into a mass of sticky and steaming inanity. Because of course all this nonsense is wholly a male thing: ask yourself – have you ever heard of a spice girl?

See also: DRINKING, FAST FOOD

INEDIBILIA

This does not mean things you encounter on a menu that are not to your taste; rather, it means being confronted with anything that is entirely impossible or highly disagreeable to eat. The good news is, this is a rare occurrence … but it has happened to me on a few occasions, and it is more than likely that it has happened to you as well, if only the once. Inedibilia will generally mean that the food is literally bad: the whiffy fish or prawn, the blue bread, the curdled cream, the rancid butter, the meat that is as high as the stars. There is absolutely no excuse whatsoever for this: the head waiter or proprietor should be summoned immediately, and challenged. And then – no matter what you are offered by way of compensation – you really ought to leave. Any kitchen that can serve up such stuff, any restaurant that will allow it to leave the pass, is simply not to be trusted any further. Whether you publicize the restaurant's failure is up to you – but people ought certainly to be made aware of any potential health hazard.

Much more common is food that is simply so ineptly cooked, or burned, or raw, or impossibly badly judged or configured, as to render it inedible. When we order a given dish, we all have in mind an idea of what we are expecting, this slavering expectation being down to prior good experiences; and if the meal set before you bears not the slightest resemblance to this, then by all means taste it if you want to, but if it then strikes you as just indescribably bad, leave it, and complain. But do be sure that you have ordered correctly in the first place: if something is billed as being made with chillies, you cannot argue with its being very hot; if you ask for a steak to be done very well indeed, you have little recourse if it is practically incinerated. Similarly, some connoisseurs like their game to be so well hung as to seem to others to be virtually putrescent: always know precisely what you are ordering. But if your meat is just so tough that no knife can cope, the chips so oily and soggy … if the soup is stone cold, the cassoulet greasy … if the fish is cooked to a paste, the vegetables boiled to the point of disintegration … this constitutes inedibilia: you do not want to eat it, nor should you contemplate doing so – and certainly you must not be expected to pay for it. Walk away. Leave enough money to cover any drink, something for the waiter (if he was any good) … and walk away. You are still hungry, I know – but look: there will be a great restaurant elsewhere, I promise you. And possibly just around the corner.

See also: COMPLAINING, DUMPS, FOOD POISONING, HEALTH AND SAFETY, ORDERING, PASS, UNUSUAL

INTERNATIONAL FOOD

International … in that it is everywhere, while not really belonging anywhere at all. The burger, hot dog, chicken wing, wrap, baguette, crêpe or sandwich that you will find on any street corner. And then, deep within the subterranean and hummingly air-conditioned guts of all those terrible and bleakly anonymous towering glass and brassy monolithic hotels that now are ubiquitous on every continent, so you will find their top-end counterparts: chateaubriand, T-bone and fillet steak, lobster, caviar, Dover sole, oysters, smoked salmon … and particularly anything out of season, and hence brightly coloured and totally tasteless, which they can boast is offered all year round. So you will need to remind yourself whether you are in Vegas or Dubai, Chicago or Sydney, Birmingham or Majorca, because the food and drink (only the most expensive brands that everyone has heard of) will be identical to that which was served to you in the first-class seat or divan provided by the airline that fawningly flew you there. International jet-set travel and dining: they shrink the wallet and broaden the stomach, while leaving the mind quite perfectly untouched.

See also: HOTELS, SEASONAL FOOD, STEAK

INVITATIONS

These used to be cut and dried, whether delivered in person, by phone or by email, or else as a note sent by snail mail or even a full-blown engraved formal pasteboard stiffy. In all cases, the principle remained the same: someone was inviting someone else to whatever it was, and all that was required of the invitee was that he either decline with regret or accept with pleasure – and, if the latter, turn up suitably attired at the given hour to the appointed place. But lately, things have become a little blurred, and particularly among younger people, who, it appears, would rather die quite horribly than be absolutely plain, committal and straightforward about anything at all on God's green earth. 'Do you fancy popping out for a bite to eat at this riverside pub next Sunday around one-ish? There will be a few of us there.' See what I mean? It's murky, isn't it? A grey area, decidedly. Does it mean that you are invited to Sunday lunch as a guest? Or are you simply being casually informed by way of a round robin that a certain set of people will be getting together in this pub around that time, and you are welcome to pitch up there if you've nothing better to do?

Often, the 'invitation' is so throwaway and possibly universal that a response is neither required nor expected. So if the idea, date, venue and company appeal, go along by all means ... but do be prepared to pay your own way, and probably that of others as well. Be prepared, too, to be met with a vaguely surprised half-greeting and a sort-of smile, due to its having slipped everyone's mind that it was mentioned to you at all. And while you're at it, you may as well be prepared also to find no one there at all because they have all slept in or else gone off somewhere else entirely, and didn't think to tell you.

See also: ETIQUETTE, GUESTS, HOSTS

ITALIAN

Who doesn't love Italian food? If you are a fan of eating out at all – and presumably you are – then you've just got to love going out to an Italian restaurant, haven't you? Of course, it is unfortunate that long ago 'Italian' became both shorthand for and synonymous with the cheap and cheerful bowl of 'spag bol' (though, admittedly, chiefly among those who were brought up on the occasional treat of Heinz Spaghetti once all the baked beans had run out, and in later life were amazed to discover that it is not in fact mandatory for pasta to come out of a tin). We have, to be sure, come a very long way, and now there are some extremely fine Italian restaurants – authentic, and true to the cooking of the regions – although such places do tend to come at a price. As will excellent Italian wine, once you climb the list from the always-good-value Montepulcianos, Sangioveses, Valpolicellas and so on – though these do remain the best buy in most of the middling restaurants: you get a lot of easy-glugging, food-friendly and fruity wine for your money.

And it is these middling restaurants that remain the best loved: if you have a long-established family-run trattoria close to where you live, then truly you are blessed. The unsimulated warmth of the welcome bestowed upon children, of course, is quite legendary … though fellow diners will often prove to be less forgiving of the little mites' boisterous antics than the staff. Legendary too are the flirtatious waiters. Well, some would say flirtatious; others would incline towards lewd and horribly embarrassing in equal measure. But they mean no harm, as they chortlingly brandish the three-foot pepper mill right in the face of *la bella signorina*: it is in their nature, and they have learnt by now that it is more or less expected of them. Generally, women don't really seem to mind the attention, the silly titillation: the older ones actually appear to love it – always providing that the waiter is youthful, slim, tanned and with thick black curly hair and a smile that would blind you. Any hint of lasciviousness from one who is old, fat, bald and sweaty, however, and they might well be moved to summon the *carabinieri*.

Nor do we mind the giant cliché that is the traditional old-fashioned Italian restaurant. Indeed, it can all be a great comfort: the red and green cloths, those ancient Chianti bottles in their raffia baskets (even better, some would insist, if charged with an age-old coagulation of candle wax), Kodachrome pictures of the Bay of Sorrento (murals even better), ritual Parmesan-sprinkling, an escalope Milanese and the lure of tiramisu. And while the ladies are gigglingly responding to the blandishments of Sylvio and Carlo and Marcello, then chaps of a certain age will enjoy nothing more than being bullied into finishing up every single last one of their *zucchini fritti* by a stern-faced, plump and unforgiving mama.

See also: **CHILDREN, DECOR, FAMILY MEALS, PIZZA, SERVICE, VALUE, WINE LIST**

This chic and attractive young woman from the 1950s
seems not to have quite mastered the art of spaghetti-twirling,
approaching the thing more as the Chinese will their bowls of noodles.
But look: she's so very chic and attractive, it matters not a jot.

Or: dress code. And that very phrase – it does appear so terribly quaint, doesn't it? So prim, so dated, quite as buttoned-up as a double-breasted blazer. But it exists still – even if often invertedly – and it's therefore as well to know one's way around it. 'Jacket required' is the most usual term employed, these days, implying as it does that while shirtsleeves and T-shirts (on their own) are not acceptable, the wearing of a tie is unnecessary. Other times you will see 'jacket and tie required' – which has the benefit of making things clear – although outside of gentlemen's clubs, an actual suit is rarely specified (unless, of course, morning dress or black or white tie, which will be plainly stipulated on a formal invitation). Often, a restaurant will appear quite careless as to what a man chooses to wear on his top half, but there will be a printed or online 'request' for him to refrain from wearing jeans or trainers. That's about as mild as it gets – unless we are going to mention those pubs and greasy spoons that, on the door, strongly discourage 'workmen's boots'.

It's all rather odd, this. There was a time when a man would always have worn a suit and tie to lunch or dinner – and the common knowledge and blanket acceptance of that was really most welcome because it completely wiped out the need for thought, a state of being that all men will embrace. Women, indeed, were envious: they had to decide (as still they do) what would or would not be too dressy (long or short, heels or not, décolleté or respectable), how best to accessorize, the degree of dazzle for jewellery … quite apart from the all-important business of remembering exactly which outfit was pressed into service on the previous comparable occasion so as not to appear as one who has simply not a single thing to wear. While all the bloke had to do was bung on a suit, knot a tie, and he was done. But now it is the man too who is left to wonder, and usually the quandary may be summed up thus: a tie or not a tie – that is the question.

And here is where the modern invertedness comes in: some places actively discourage a tie because they seem to have decided that here is the absolute epitome of 'stuffy', while many men are equally desperate to be seen to be laid back and cool (and therefore by implication, they must hope most earnestly, youthful) – and further, they now have been indoctrinated into thinking of the tie as an emblem of work, if not abject enslavement. Everyone nurtures an absolute horror of appearing overdressed, while the concept of underdressing would appear to be perfectly extinct. Myself, I cannot understand this: it is no hardship whatsoever to wear a tie, and it provides a grand opportunity to add a little smidgen of oomph and colour to something otherwise humdrum. Though if you do not intend to sport a tie, then it is a good idea not to go with a shirt that is designed to be worn with one – i.e. virtually all shirts, unless they be collarless ('grandad') or stand-up cylindrical ('Nehru'). The cravat could be seen to be a rather splendid compromise, but for some reason or other it has long ago been collectively decided that such a thing is an utter laughing stock (no pun intended, but it's there if you want it). One yearns to be a vicar, sometimes (not often), if only to obviate the dilemma – though taking the cloth simply in order to sidestep the risk of any sartorial solecism might just be a little extreme.

Really, it all comes down to manners: dressing in a way that makes everyone else feel comfortable, although not to the extent that you altogether go against your natural inclinations – one does not wish to be a sheep. As a general rule of thumb, ladies should avoid T-shirts bearing slogans that make it difficult for people not to engage openly upon the reading of their bosom – as well as anything, indeed, that transcends mildly sexy and plunges headlong and neckline into really quite ridiculously provocative. It is also polite at any meal worthy of the name not to load up on the perfume: too much Opium or Mitsouko and the subtlety of sauces, the bouquet of wine, go straight out of the window. And gentlemen? Apart from not looking like a scruff when your lady friend is all dressed up (terribly common, alas), here is the cardinal rule: whatever else you do, just for pity's sake keep yourself covered. We don't want bare arms, and obviously not legs (well Christ, what are you thinking about? Obviously not *legs*: unless you are at the beach, shorts are absolutely out – and the same is true of sandals). What else? No headgear of any description … and, on balance, the display of a tangle of chest hair is really best kept among two consenting adults.

See also: ETIQUETTE, FORMAL DINNERS, GLAMOUR, GUESTS, HOSTS, INVITATIONS

KITCHEN TABLE

The kitchen in a restaurant used to be something you took completely for granted: there was one, obviously – possibly subterranean – and should you think of it at all, you simply hoped to goodness that it was cleanly scrubbed and generally well run, while trying your hardest not to dwell upon all the tales that you had concentrated so very hard not to hear in the past, all of them concerning the myriad of appalling crimes against hygiene that in restaurant kitchens were ritually and habitually committed, these to include the juxtaposition of cooked and raw things, rodents, the blood from a commis chef's finger and the methods of malevolent vengeance grimly wrought by terminally aggrieved and ill-paid underlings. But these days the kitchen has emerged from the shadows: it is out there and proud! A great big slice of wall has been removed from the flank of many of our more fashionable restaurants so that snatches of a glinting and stainless-steel universe beyond may be glimpsed by the eager punter – a mighty strange land of greenish mists, of sizzle and appalling clatter, and one that is peopled by red-faced and shiny men and women in whites, each of them topped off by an abbreviated toque. And so now – suddenly, and at a stroke – that lousy table next to the swing door to the kitchen (the only two lousier being that by the entrance, a spot subject to one hell of a draught every time the door is opened, and that other one, you know the one, the one by the loos – quite enough said) … this has become the place to be: dinner and theatre, all in one go!

And soon after that, the concept was expanded – or it was in some of the rather posher places anyway, those with chefs that everyone had heard of. You can visualize the brainstorming session as the idea for a brand-new frontier, a brand-new fashion, gradually came to be hatched: 'Hey, listen to this, everybody – how about a table not just next to the kitchen, but actually *inside* it? How about that?' '*In* the kitchen …? *In* the kitchen …? What – so as to squeeze in more paying customers when we're extra busy, do you mean?' 'No – to have it as a nightly feature. Lunchtimes too.' 'I see … and make it a loss-leader sort of a thing? Bang it out cheap, with a bit of an apology and a buckshee glass of Prosecco?' 'On the contrary: big it up to be the most unique, exclusive and highly sought-after opportunity for no more than six or eight or maybe just a dozen people to see, smell and hear our genius chefs up close and personal – and I'm thinking aloud here, but how about we bung in an endless tasting menu and charge the bloody earth? What do you think?' 'Hmm … sounds like a plan. Let's go for it, baby!'

And so it came to pass. Purely a matter of personal taste, all of this, of course – although it has certainly proved to be a popular idea, particularly among parties of foodies on a special night out. For myself, I prefer a comfortable table in the quiet and warm embrace of the restaurant proper, while the cooks remain at their stations in the kitchen: a place for everything, you see? And everything in its place.

See also: BOOKING, DECOR, FASHION, MENUS, STAR CHEFS, TABLES

LADIES WHO LUNCH

There's this gag about a lady who goes to see a doctor about an abiding stomach complaint and recurring headaches. 'Do you take a drink with your meals?' he asks her. She is properly aghast: 'Take a drink with my meals …?! Certainly not. Why – I don't even take any *food* with my meals!' And so the legend goes: a gaggle of lavish ladies with no very specially pressing appointments, duties or involvements who cluster to form a beautifully dressed, coiffed and painted ensemble at a table in one of the more fashionable restaurants, their very expensively shod feet generally obscured by a glorious clutter of terribly smart and glossy carrier bags – the sort that bear illustrious Bond Street names, and have coloured rope handles. Their orders will usually involve a Dover sole and a glass or two of something cold and white. A very famous supermodel is often to be spotted in one of my favourite London restaurants: she toys with the sole, drinks a fair deal of Veuve Clicquot and frequently nips out around the back for a Marlboro Light (a pack of which, along with her iPhone and a Dunhill lighter, is never far from her fingers) – at least four or five fag breaks by the time I've seen off a *fritto misto* and am well into a large fish pie.

A man can become visibly upset if he has brought a recent female acquaintance to a painfully expensive restaurant and she orders something such as Dover sole or lobster, and then proceeds merely to idle with it: a chap will generally enjoy to see a woman tucking in with gusto (yes, and especially if he is paying for it). The exception, however, would appear to be Lord Byron, not just a ladies' man of unimpeachable repute, but clearly – as may be seen from the following quotation – the sadly uncanonized patron saint of ladies who lunch: 'A woman should never be seen eating or drinking, unless it be lobster salad and champagne, the only true feminine and becoming viands.' You can see why they loved him so much.

Perhaps it is merely that men are just the more natural lunchers? For the truth is that for many women, when they all get together for a hen-only gathering – be it lunch, book club or Ann Summers party (because they can't still be doing Tupperware, can they?) – the point of the exercise is rarely to be discovered in nourishment, literature or sex; rather, it is simply to do with a good old natter. They just like to talk to one another, is all, which is no bad thing. Men don't really understand this – nor how two women can be on the phone for upwards of twenty minutes simply in order to arrange a rendezvous in a restaurant so that the two of them can have a jolly good chat. And another thing that men don't understand is when women gleefully quote Kate Moss: 'Nothing tastes as good as skinny feels.' Here is a foreign language.

See also: FASHION, LUNCH, ROMANCE, SMOKING, SPECIAL REQUIREMENTS

LE PATRON MANGE ICI

And so I should bloody well hope! Because if the patron doesn't mange ici, actually, then where the hell does he mange? And why do we mange here, then? Why don't we all go and mange wherever he is?

LIQUID LUNCH

We keep being told that this ancient and glorious institution is a thing of the past – and, to a very large extent, one has to concede that this is sadly true. But who can remember the days when a highly paid Fleet Street hack, say, would file his copy (always immaculate, no matter how gruellingly alcohol-sodden the preceding night) by midday at the latest, this leaving him free to amble down the road in like and jolly company to somewhere such as El Vino's … a couple of gin and tonics, large ones, maybe three … sharing a bottle or so of Chablis with the fish, a couple of claret at least with the meat … and then as many ports or brandies with cigars or cigarettes as could

An Edwardian victim of a rather severe case of *le vin triste*.
Only moments before, all was very jolly indeed … and then,
rather suddenly, it hit him between the eyes. It was
that fifth bottle – that's where he went wrong.

decently be accommodated until it was suddenly time for the sun-over-the-yardarm first-of-the-evening snifter of maybe a pint, or else a Scotch and soda … on and on into the night, it went. Often, the food part was omitted altogether. And then they'd drive home – to a man being possessed of the unshakeable belief that of course they drove much better when they'd had one or two, and never mind that the first twenty minutes of the attempt would be taken up solely with the business of inserting the key into the door lock. But the following morning, they would once again file immaculate copy.

Yes, well: they're all dead now, those heroic veteran tipplers, and for fairly obvious reasons. But still there are pockets of liquid lunch-dom that linger on tenaciously: in politics or the services, say, or publishing and the film business. And in gentlemen's clubs, where many remain of the view that it is what afternoons were made for. Not to say more generally at Christmas and a cluster of other high days and holidays, when out a boat ought certainly to be pushed. And if you study the calendar with due and proper application, there is usually to be discovered some or other thing that can give rise to cele-bration, if you're sufficiently determined.

See also: BAR, CELEBRATIONS, CHRISTMAS, CLUBS, DESIGNATED DRIVER, DRINKING, LUNCH, WEDDINGS, WINE LIST

LITTLE PLATES

It's tapas that are to blame, of course, for the apparently unstoppable spread and just-so-thrilling fashionability of this phenomenon. Then came Italian *cichetti* … and, I suppose, thinking about it, the Chinese have been doing the things for millennia. One can see the appeal: everyone chowing down to a fine assortment of delectable titbits. Because obviously, here is an option only if there is a group of you: it doesn't work nearly so well with just a couple. Having said that, I was once stood up by some woman or other for lunch in a tapas bar, so it turned out that there was only little me ... but I ordered everything for two anyway, and revelled in the luxury of not having to exercise restraint and politeness by leaving the last of three of my very favourite morsels (they often come in threes), but instead just wolfing it down in a wilful act of glorious and piggy selfishness.

Little plates, tapas ... Along with street food impetuously grabbed at, they never really were intended to be fully-fledged lunches or dinners, but simply a selection of flavoursome savoury nibbles to aid the absorption of either a marathon drinking session, or else sustained and determined sipping throughout the afternoon. But the sheer informality and sometimes rather self-conscious quasi-spontaneity of the whole idea has caught on in a very big way, and particularly among the young (for whom no occasion may ever be said to be too informal – and all the better if you have to queue in the rain to get into the place due to a no-bookings policy and the seating is bloody uncomfortable, the lighting dim, the music raucous). Know this: most places pride themselves on delivering individual dishes to your table whenever they damn well please, whether this does or doesn't coincide with the order in which you might prefer to eat them. And you should also be aware that although each of the prices might seem very seductively low on the menu – they are, after all, only little plates – you will need simply loads of the things if a proper lunch or dinner is the general idea, along with gallons of drink to while away the intervals between the serving on a whim of this, that or the other ... and so the meal will never end up being the absolute bargain that it first might well have appeared.

See also: DRINKING, FAST FOOD, OUTDOOR EATING, QUEUING, VALUE, YOUNG PLACES

LONDON

While it is sometimes hard to remember that New York is not in fact the capital of the United States, with Paris and London there can never be any doubt: here are capital cities writ large, with no competition. And in the old days, if anyone was required to cite the capital city that was by far the most attuned to cuisine, the place that boasted the finest and most famous restaurants in the world ... well, then it was Paris, obviously: no contest. But now, while still from the French there would be no debate (national pride, *vive la France* and all that sort of thing), many would unhesitatingly name London as the restaurant capital of the world. Of course, Paris can still be absolutely wonderful – though you do have to be willing to lay down a total bloody fortune if you truly want the best. New York, it need hardly be said, is no slouch either – many very fine places there. But London, well ... the sheer number and bewildering diversity of restaurants at every single level is not just overwhelming on the one hand, but also, on the other, extremely gratifying.

On the very highest rung of the ladder, London now indisputably does excel. And nor is the scene ever static: just as the established greats continue to consolidate their justified eminence, so are new and exciting places with extremely talented chefs and professional service opening all the time. Of course, the very best are expensive – but still at least not Paris expensive, never quite that. And in Britain, readers of the national press will often become disgruntled with restaurant reviewers who continue to pay homage to London to the detriment and exclusion, as they see it, of the whole of the rest of the country. But face it: if a professionally backed brilliant new venture, maybe featuring a great star chef, is about to be opened ... well, it ain't going to be happening in Newcastle, or Reading, or Wells-next-the-Sea. Is it? Here is simply a fact. London rules – London is swinging! Whatever Paris may say.

See also: BUZZ, FASHION, FRENCH, RESTAURANT REVIEWS, STAR CHEFS

LOOS

By law, a restaurant must have them. Management and Health and Safety inspectors, in theory, will ensure their cleanliness and functionality. So therefore it follows that all restaurant loos must be equal, right? Mmm … well I don't really have to respond to rhetoric that is not so much flawed as riddled with buckshot – for as well we all know, they vary. Oh my God, how they vary. One of the chief pleasures remaining in dining in a hotel is the fact that you just know that the loos will be spacious, up to date and well maintained (because I'm assuming that you wouldn't be going to the sort of flea-bag hotel where they aren't). But modern and fashionable restaurants have truly upped the game to a remarkable degree: so lavish are the facilities in some of them that I constantly am amazed that the quarries in Italy and China still can have any trace of marble left in them. Add to that the blinding-white deco-style porcelain made sparkly by the recessed downlights, the wink of gleaming chrome, the glossy bottles of Molton Brown and occasionally even Floris … heavens, sometimes you just want to pack a bag and move in permanently.

The best of them will have little individual fluffy white hand towels, which you toss with nonchalance into an Ali Baba basket, once you are done. The loop of towelling on a wooden roller – which thankfully these days is very seldom seen – was never a nice idea (the germs, they just kept on rotating, round and round they went; quite a lucky dip as to just which strain of bacteria Mistress Fortune had you slated to contract). The huge roller towels on a drum within a dispenser are fine, although you need the strength of Samson to tug down on the things – and sometimes you tug in vain, for the towel has reached its journey's end, and no one has come along to replace it. But even paper towels, in my view, are infinitely preferable to the electric hand-dryer. And particularly if there is only one of the whiningly roaring things, and a queue of doleful people are just simply left standing there, dripping from the fingers. And even more particularly if it's one of those Dyson Airblades, which are becoming increasingly common. You stick your hands into them – okay, yes, I can grasp the concept so far – but I am never completely confident that I shall be able to withdraw them again with all ten digits still in place: I think it's because the device reminds me irresistibly of a shredder.

What people no longer seem to appreciate is he who used to be called a lavatory attendant. A mute and understandably deeply bored gentleman (or lady, I suppose – I wouldn't know: I don't these days get into the Ladies as much as I'd like to) in a white cotton jacket and thinking about Christ alone knows what all day long as he hands a towel to this person, proffers a clothes brush to that. People are not too happy any more with this kind of service … and nor are they happy at the sight of that accusatory saucer brimming with pound coins (though if one is there, do for God's sake add to their number: just look at the poor sod – it's the least you can do).

But all restaurant loos are not like this. Within just the last year (admittedly in my capacity as a restaurant reviewer) I have been in some that have actually appalled me: damp and blistered walls, floor awash with water – and from whence it came you do not care to ponder. And over the years I have encountered slivers of slimy soap. No soap. Grubby towel. No towel. Paper-towel dispensers: empty. Electric dryers covered in black and yellow Sellotape proclaiming their out-of-orderness. Lavatory bowls in an unspeakable state. Flushes that don't. Loose seats. No seats. Thin and scratchy paper. No paper. Locks on the cubicle doors that are hanging on by a thread. No locks. Streaked and mottled mirror, crack'd from side to side. Smashed mirror. No mirror. Good God … how can all this be allowed to happen? I am told that things are always considerably better in the Ladies (I wouldn't know: I don't these days get into the Ladies as much as I'd like to), but then on the downside there never seem to be sufficient facilities in the Ladies, and hence the eternal and embarrassed queue stretching way past the door, many of the queuers really quite flushed, and contorting their limbs.

And am I alone in simply loathing 'jokey' names on the doors? While the simple word 'lavatory' seems no longer to exist, even Gentlemen and Ladies are becoming a rarity. But we can surely do without Guys and Gals, Bulls and Cows – can't we? Cocks and Hens, Beaux and Belles … and I swear that I have also seen the following: Vicars and Tarts, Man of the House and The Little Woman, Bogart and Bacall. Lordy, Lordy. Though I think the most offensive of all are Male Toilet and Female Toilet, but maybe that's just me. Similarly, you yourself will refer to the 'loo' – nothing crude, such as 'bog'; nothing twee, such as 'little girl's room' – and never must you dream of using either of the perfectly ridiculous transatlantic euphemisms: I have always thought that if all these Americans truly do feel in need of a room in which to have a bath or a rest slap bang in the middle of lunch, well then they'll just have to bloody well wait till later, and have them both at home.

Okay, enough – here endeth the effusion, and I apologize if it was over fulsome … but look: it's better out than in.

LUNCH

At the risk of appearing to be a damned and literal fool, just let me say this: lunch is not dinner. And the truth of it is never more apparent than when in a restaurant, where the distinctions are acute. By lunchtime, you already will have done something or other with your day – whether pleasurable or not, strenuous or otherwise – so still you ought to be reasonably fresh and alert. And, unless it is a liquid lunch or a romantic lunch, probably you are intending to do a further something or other afterwards. So there is, you see, a tacit cut-off point, which, rather wonderfully, generally is subliminally hit upon by all concerned, and more or less simultaneously.

Dinner, therefore, is different: all that might be achieved that day is behind you – you might be happy, frustrated, anxious or even quite utterly knackered, yearning for an early night and dreading the busi-ness of bathing, changing and bloody going out again. At lunch, this shouldn't be the case – and if it is, you really do need to get a grip. Lunch can be as light, fleeting and inexpensive as you like … or it can be a lengthy and glorious indulgence. It can be outdoors, in a cafe, up at the bar, or even on the hoof (should you actually wish it to be a movable feast). It is, in short, the most versatile and delightful meal of the day, with none of the foregone conventions nor expecta-tions that come with dinner (nor, come to that, breakfast or tea). And it is almost certainly going to be less expensive: you'll find a bargain lunch, rarely a bargain dinner. And because it is always less formal, you can get away with inviting just the relevant (or attractive) person whom you actually want to talk to, without feeling obliged to drag in all the right-hand men and spouses into the equation – tricky to pull this off at dinner. So: lunch can truly be all things to all men. Lunch is a wonder. Lunch is the closest I come to formal religion: and for that much, let us all join hands in saying grace, and offering up our thanks.

See also: BARGAIN LUNCH, BREAKFAST, BUSINESS LUNCH, DINNER, LIQUID LUNCH, ROMANCE, TEA

MENUS

If you are lunching or dining in one of your regularly occasional haunts, there is little so comforting as the sight of the menu, because you just know it's going to be exactly the same as the last time you were here – and anyway, you barely have to glance at it because you have already decided that you are going to order the very same things that you ordered the last time you were here, because of course you order the very same things every single time you come here: that's what regularly occasional haunts are for. So it will send tremors down the spine if that menu has indeed undergone changes, as occasionally happens – and particularly if it means that the very same things you always order are no longer there! Such upheaval can prove to be seismic, and might easily result in the place being struck off your list. More likely, though, is just the odd slipped-in little hike in prices, which – along with your favourite grub – you just must swallow.

The joy of a menu in an unfamiliar restaurant is all to do with hungry anticipation: hmm … what have we here, then? Of course, one always has an idea of the sort of menu it will be, but I always make a point of not looking it up online beforehand because then the first sight of the actual menu that you are hotly clutching can prove something of a let-down. The type of menu that has completely fallen out of favour – except in the grand hotels that invented it, along with all sorts of misguided and pretentious provincial places that still are vainly clinging to the coat-tails of 1959 – is that which resembles a padded-leather wedding photograph album, most often replete with rope and tassels. This, together with a similarly bound and infinitely thicker wine list, was generally intended to assure the assured (who, by definition, were requiring no such assurance) that here was truly a place to be reckoned with, while at the same time (highly gratifyingly to both the maître d' and sommelier) scaring the novice witless. Rather more welcome these days is a simple printed card bearing that day's date: this indicates an ever-changing daily menu that is driven by the market and comprises – in theory – the best of what is currently available. So long as they don't become all rather nuts and flowery with the language, talking about some damn thing or other having been lovingly gathered by hand at the crack of a beautiful dawn by an even more beautiful virgin, born to the purpose – you know exactly the sort of twaddle I mean. There is always the chance in such a place, of course, that none of that day's offerings will appeal … but it's a long chance, really. Rather more likely is that they quickly run out of the favourite – so get your order in fast.

Some established and very 'in' places exercise a little *jeu d'esprit* upon their customers: the famous dish that people travel miles to slaver over does not appear on the menu. J. Sheekey, the great London fish restaurant, used to do this with its legendary fishcakes. I knew of a marvellous Italian restaurant in Soho that pulled the same gag with its renowned and world-class seafood linguine – and until very recently, Joe Allen in Covent Garden, one of London's original and best American diners, actually had the tremendous wit and gall to omit from its menu the very cheeseburger that in those days was known by everyone to be the very best in town by a mile. In every case the dish was of course available … you just had to know to ask for it. And, once more, this thrills all those who are in the loop, while bewildering everyone else: the basis of this country's class structure, fundamentally.

And then there is the blackboard – which is fine if you can read it from afar, a thing I never seem to manage. But menus of any description are always a bit worrying if they are constantly all-embracing and utterly massive: so many varieties of food means it just cannot be fresh, and that the restaurant will simply defrost to order. By contrast, the choice on some bargain-lunch menus can be very narrow indeed – but this does almost guarantee freshness, and this is always important. And if nothing appeals, there is always the carte. Not to say … the tasting menu. This makes quite regular appearances in the higher sort of place that boasts a star chef, and often is the reason why people will make a point of going there. At its best, it is

It might be worth noting that the prices chalked up
outside this New York restaurant of the late 1930s are all in cents,
not dollars. Nonetheless, this poor devil seems to be summing up the
pros and cons. Or maybe he's just catching up on his reading.

a leisurely journey of gastronomic revelation serving to rouse from their hibernation taste buds you were barely aware you possessed. Rather more often, though, it is merely an exercise in preening and muscle-flexing on the part of the kitchen – rather in the manner of an actress's portfolio of greatest hits, replete with the critics' encomia. The waiter will talk you through each little morsel, and you are constantly expected to applaud. Apart from the expense, the real disappointment comes in the form of the very word 'tasting'. You are not at a tasting, are you? You are meant to be having dinner. So ask yourself: three courses of your choice? Or between twelve and thirty little soupçons devised for your palate's titillation by a self-styled genius? The choice is always there.

Some people collect menus: they will ask to take one home (or even nick it). This happens less in these days of online everything (reviewers would ritually request a menu because it saved them all the beastly bother of writing anything down), though restaurants are never that keen on the idea, unless it is simply a daily printed sheet. Well-produced menus cost money … but they are usually sympathetic if here is a big and memorable night out, and someone is merely seeking a tangible souvenir. Famous restaurants go through sheaves of the things, and particularly should certain star chefs be on a sufficiently long break from making television programmes and endorsing their ghosted magazine pieces to have made time actually to spend a moment on the premises: their signatures on the menu will be prized. And a restaurant will always be eager to indulge a one-off diner who seems to mean business … because after all – who knows? It might encourage him to become a regular occasional who then will always order the very same things that he ordered the last time he was here.

See also: BARGAIN LUNCH, KITCHEN TABLE, OFF MENU, ORDERING, REGULAR HAUNTS, STAR CHEFS, THEFT

I can well understand the thinking behind it: dear old mum, she's been slaving away for us all year long, cooking non-stop – the least we can do is take her out for lunch on Mother's Day and show her just how much we all appreciate her. Well … this might have washed in the days when mothers all seemed to be fairly ancient from the very day they first gave birth, had no jobs, outside interests nor labour-saving devices, and rarely went out of the front door unless it was to scrub the step, or else a trip to the bakers or the bins, and therefore seldom thought it worth their while to remove the pins and curlers; so for Mother's Day she can get a perm and bring out that lovely rose-pink cardigan that she keeps for best and have a right old beano. But it's so not like that now – well is it? Mums are ever youthful and cap-able, often with responsible jobs that involve a fair deal of dining out anyway, and would far rather be left alone to enjoy the day as they please (having already had to cope with the well-meaning horror of breakfast in bed, the highlight of which was not the massacre of egg, but a dandelion in a jam jar). So among all the mums who ritually are hauled off to some place or other on Mother's Day, the treat tends really to be levelled at either the very young and yummy mummys who just recently have given birth (so the twelve-year-olds and upwards, then) or else the grandmas. So often there can be three or four mothers at the table, God knows how many children and grand-children, and the one glum bloke who knows he's going to be paying for it all (and nor does that situation alter one jot when he in turn, poor sod, is dragged out for Father's Day).

Along with all the other Great Days that have been invented and endlessly propagated by Hallmark, it's a hellish time to be lunch-ing anywhere – and if you don't believe me, just take a look around the restaurant: it's chock-full of harassed and embarrassed mums trying their damnedest to be grateful and mumsy, teenagers who on this bright Sunday afternoon charged with potential just yearn to be anywhere else on earth but here, babies who are bawling … and the one glum bloke who knows he's going to be paying for it all. Restaurants of every description just love it, of course: the top hotel dining rooms are fully booked, and so are the local trattorias. Such chains as Harvester and Toby Carvery can hardly believe their luck: packed to the gills. Cakes will make an appearance, and so will ripples of applause and even single red roses within cellophane tubes. Glasses will be raised, and drink will be drunk … except by the designated driver, of course – and that will be the one glum bloke who knows he's going to be paying for it all.

See also: CELEBRATIONS, CHILDREN, CHRISTMAS, DESIGNATED DRIVER, FAMILY MEALS, NEW YEAR'S EVE, VALENTINE'S DAY

MUSIC

Or so we call it, for want of a more accurate term. For I am not now talking of venues where the live music is the very point: a piano bar, if you fancy a little bit of a relaxing tinkle … or Ronnie Scott's Jazz Club in Soho, say, where they will serve you a more than adequate dinner while you are heavily into being a hep cool cat, or whatever it is you imagine yourself to be doing. But in such context, the dinner is hardly the most important thing. If you go to any sort of stage show, revue or variety act, then that's why you are there: the food will usually be adequate, the drink extortionate. This seems to be particularly true with burlesque, where anyway the food tends to be left to get cold. These, however, are the exceptions: in most cases, canned music ('muzak', we used to say) is foisted upon you whether you like it or not … and if you don't like it, then you really shouldn't be there.

Levels of obnoxiousness vary, of course – as can one's levels of tolerance. In a gastropub – where the music is always, but always, the whim of whomever happens to be working the bar, and to hell with the paying customer – it really doesn't matter too much unless it is

We are in Rome, and it is 1955. The meal is done,
the cigarettes are lit; it has been an oh-so-heavenly evening.
And then … the serenaders arrive, this resulting in at least
one of the party slumping into a coma.

so damn loud that no conversation whatsoever is possible … because you're not actually going to be there that long (in my own case, about thirty seconds ought to do it), and presumably on this occasion food isn't the primary business – and you're in a gastropub, for God's sake, so what do you expect? Where it matters very much is in a 'proper' restaurant. You can always, of course, request that they turn it down, and usually they will comply with this; they might, if you are inordinately fortunate, even turn it off altogether – though never if there is some or other spotty little nerd around to officiously lecture you at length on the endlessly compelling topic of 'company policy'. But when the volume is lowered, this can often have the effect of leaving solely the throbbing bass line to insinuate itself evilly into the innermost crannies of your brain, there to lodge forever. Just leave. Why suffer? Just leave. If you want to go mad, there are quicker and cheaper ways (a picnic springs to mind). One great truth is this, however: really good restaurants never, ever play music. Full stop.

See also: CONVERSATION, GASTROPUBS

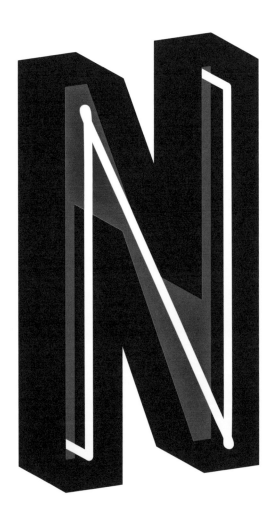

NAMES OF RESTAURANTS

Time was when restaurants, like shops, were named after the owner who ran them – and often, in the case of Italian places in particular, this would take the possessive form: Gennaro's, Quaglino's, Manzi's, Bertorelli's and so on. This idea returned in a flurry during the late 1980s and 1990s when the star chefs first emerged from the chrysalis in order to flutter so colourfully: Marco Pierre White, Gordon Ramsay – all the usual suspects. This was fine when they each had but the one restaurant and could be relied upon to be slaving away in the kitchen, but how long did that last? The public are not utter fools: if there are ten restaurants all touting a single chef's name, in how many of these can he actually be cooking? Well, by the time it gets to this stage, the answer is almost certainly none: he's far too busy making television programmes, buying Bentleys, signing off on ghosted cookbooks and sitting on a yacht. As soon as chefs become over-promoted (in both senses of the term), they simply cease to cook. Then there were all the restaurants with defiantly French names, and these tend to hail from a time when French unequivocally equalled great: L'Escargot, La Poule au Pot, L'Epicure, L'Etoile, A L'Ecu de France … More recently we have a fashion for single, rather meaningless words: Cut, Apostrophe, Ark, this sort of thing. And most maddening of all: numbers. The number of the building in a street, most usually – but deftly omitting the name of the street itself. So woe betide you if you simply cannot remember whether you are due to meet people at 34 … or 85 … or some other bloody number altogether.

See also: STAR CHEFS

NEW YEAR'S EVE

Don't. Is my basic advice. I know that around October it can sometimes appear to be a rather good idea, but honestly, listen to me: it isn't. Just don't. And do I really have to go into all the rigmarole of actually telling you why …? Oh well all right then: all the best restaurants and hotels will be booked, and the ones that are not fully booked, or even partially booked, you really do not want to go to. And if one or two of the best places do have tables to offer, these will very likely come in the form of 'executive packages' – and these are not, as you might have expected, a selection of drones plucked from middle management trussed up roughly in string and brown paper, but simply a bundle of PR guff optimistically attempting to disguise something really very ordinary, the cost of which will probably entail the selling of your house. And every restaurant, of whatever quality, will be packing in extra tables – so you will be cheek by jowl with perfect strangers who are not just far from perfect but also glassy-eyed and seemingly rabid in their determination TO ALL HAVE A REALLY GOOD TIME!

There will be balloons. There will be those unspeakable things with a little feather on the end that people blow through and into your face, this resulting in a rude and cacophonous rasp that the perpetrators evidently believe to be quite intensely amusing, for they will do it again. And again. There will be 'party poppers', which means that all your food and drink will have all sorts of glittery little bits in it. There will be champagne at prices you have never before witnessed. And once dinner is over and you are contemplating the chocolate mint melting in a rather Dali-esque manner in your coffee saucer, there will be a great deal of hanging about because midnight is still just bleeding ages away, and so what are you supposed to do but drink? Champagne, probably – at prices you have never before witnessed. Though many diners by now will have drifted on to the hard stuff – cognac, vodka, Tia Maria – whereupon they will glow and shine as if from an inner purple light, and become just a little demented and more resolved than ever TO HAVE A REALLY GOOD TIME!

And such roaring, giddy people will be interspersed with women who are weeping – because for every joyous woman who is floating on a cloud not only because of the Chardonnay but also for the reason that they have just been proposed to and the engagement ring had been concealed very disgustingly within a crème caramel, some other woman will be weeping, and probably unable to tell you quite why, it's just that on this night of the year she always becomes reflective about all the years and people gone by and fearful of what this brand-new one might have in store for her ... and so as a result of that and all the Baileys, she cries her bloody eyes out. And then the bongs will strike and everyone goes briefly insane and if you're not very careful indeed you are going to get kissed, and never by that gorgeous person down at the end there upon whom you have had your eye for quite some considerable time. Then there will be more drink because it's only once a year after all and Christmas now is finally over and soon it will be noses to the grindstone but on the bright side no one has to get up early and go in to work tomorrow morning (oh but what are you saying?! It *is* tomorrow morning!) and then quite suddenly a cold and collective premature hangover will descend upon the entire company. And people now feel weary, and sour-mouthed, and grubby, and drunk, and stupid, and are trying not even to *think* about the bill, which they idly suppose they now might as well just get out of the way. And if you really think you are then just going to be able to saunter out into the drizzle (there will be drizzle) and hail a passing taxi ... well, all I can say is: stroll on, matey (which, quite literally, you will be compelled to do).

So. Just. Don't.

See also: CELEBRATIONS, CHRISTMAS, DRINKING, VALUE

NOSE TO TAIL

The phrase was popularized by way of the title of a cookbook written by the eminent chef Fergus Henderson, he of St John fame. St John is a restaurant close to London's Smithfield Market that specializes in utterly fresh British meat, fish and game, unmucked about. Astonishingly, it has garnered a Michelin star – the astonishment arising not because of the quality of the cooking, which is high, but because of the decor: for there is none, you see. The Michelin people traditionally are very insistent on all the trappings of fine dining before they go doling out stars, but what we have in St John is a sterile white box with a concrete floor and coldly lit by metal pendants as last seen in a wartime factory: cheap white paper on the tables, the crudest glassware and cutlery, service that may truthfully be said to be casual – and the only nod to decoration of any description being down to whether a diner should choose to hang up his coat or hat on one of the bare wooden pegs sticking out from the wall.

And so, seamlessly in tune with so severely puritan an ethic, Fergus decreed that no part of an animal should be wasted or ignored: not just the prime cuts would be offered, but all the unspeakable bits as well. This, of course, is what very poor people with smallholdings have been doing for centuries: a pig might have to feed a family for a year – there could be no question of waste, and hence black pudding and trotters. But here was the intriguing question: would diners at what is actually one of London's most expensive restaurants be willing to sometimes eschew the fillet and best end and chow down instead on a brimming bowlful of tail, or else maybe a fine big plate of nose? Well, it worked – and of course other restaurants were quick and eager to follow the example: if punters are happy to part with a very fair whack of the folding stuff in exchange for all the ghastly detritus that we used to just heave into the bin, well then who are we to discourage them? Pâtés and terrines have long been loved by restaurants for the very same reason – and the same is true of soups and pies: money in the bank, all of them.

See also: DECOR, FASHION, OVERHEADS, RESTAURANT GUIDES, STAR CHEFS, VALUE

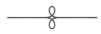

OFF MENU

Ordering off menu is seen in some quarters to be a rather cool thing to do. Such people will talk of 'testing the kitchen' by asking for something that does not appear listed, or else requesting that some or other ingredient that does feature on the menu be cooked in a completely different way. And with another sauce. Well look: it's all a bit unnecessary really, isn't it? Don't you think? Menus are usually perfectly adequate – but if you truly cannot find there a single thing you want to eat and so feel compelled to ask for something else entirely … well then maybe you're just in the wrong restaurant. Or possibly you're just such an insufferable sod – in equal measure preening and overbearing – that you shouldn't actually be in any restaurant at all. Having said all that, it is perfectly acceptable to request tagliatelle, say, instead of spaghetti. A Béarnaise sauce in place of the listed maître d'hôtel butter or peppercorn. The vegetables from that dish with this dish. And if the restaurant agrees with pleasure, well fine … but don't push it: if they can they will, if they can't, they can't. But any decent place will be keen to accommodate the wishes of a diner, provided he limits his desires to within the bounds of the possible. Interestingly, some restaurants play the idea in reverse by pointedly not listing things that are actually available – often, rather naughtily, their signature dish, this known only to those in the know: and for more about this, please see 'Menus'.

See also: MENUS, ORDERING

ON THE WAGON

The wagon can be a perfectly fine thing to be on (as opposed to a bandwagon, which you never want even to be near), but whether you should wilfully inflict such a state upon your fellow diners … well, that is moot. Because there are happy wagoners (for which read quite appallingly smug, pious and self-congratulatory wagoners), and then there are those who are frankly and visibly undergoing hell. Neither faction should really be let loose on a band of merely normal diners, who will be enjoying a glass or two of wine: one does not wish for lectures, censure, mission statements, and nor a boring presence … though neither does one ever want to be causing pain to another by forcing him to be a witness to an orgy of forbidden fruit – bad restaurant manners, apart from anything else. Some can be on the wagon simply for a day or two, either as part of their brand-new regime of having two or more days a week off the booze ('watching the units'), or else simply because they are shakily attempting recovery from one quite glorious hell of a bender. In the case of the former, however, we require no hint whatsoever of the recent fashion for competitive non-drinking: an inversion of the old-style bragging about how utterly wasted one is rendered, night after night – this time around taking the form of crowing very tediously about how many days one has gone without booze. A little of that goes a very long way.

Non-drinking can be a permanent state too, as in the case of one who is ill, a lifelong practitioner of teetotalism, or else struggling with the daily all-out war against alcoholism. It goes without saying that such unfortunates should never, ever be urged to take a drink, joshingly or otherwise: any such taunting is rude, self-serving and inconsiderate – and might even result in their taking you up on your offer, and then where will you be? Your conscience will never let you alone. So: no one must be accused of being a 'party pooper' … though equally, no one should actually be such a thing. What it comes down to is judging the company and the nature of the event. It is completely acceptable to everyone – abstainer and indulger alike – for a member of the party at lunchtime to cleave to water or a Diet Coke (towards which the non-drinker somehow seems programmed to gravitate, later to discover its intrinsically addictive complexion). But if we are talking about a lads' night out or a celebratory evening, the non-drinker might be best advised to opt out – for his own sake, as well as that of everyone else. The abstainer should remember this: if for whatever reason you don't want booze, well fine – but just don't go on about it, that's all. The drinker should remember this: it needn't actually come down to a choice so stark as on the wagon, or off your head.

See also: BAR, CELEBRATIONS, DRINKING, LIQUID LUNCH, NEW YEAR'S EVE

OPENING HOURS

The only thing you really need to be aware of is that although a restaurant's opening hours are generally plainly stated, it doesn't always follow that they will be pleased to serve you at any time between the flinging open of their doors, and bolting them shut again for the night. If a place says it opens at noon, they may not actually relish a booking for that time – and if they do take it, you might be kept waiting while they get into gear (though all this rigmarole is far less likely in a brasserie). If you want a table for one o'clock, you might be offered 1.15 or 1.30: this isn't just to be perverse, and nor to annoy you. Most lunchers unthinkingly plump for one o'clock – because it's lunchtime, right? – and so often a restaurant will try to stagger the bookings in order not to overwhelm the kitchen with simultaneous orders. As ever, if 1.15 or 1.30 is fine … then fine. If not, continue to press your claim for one o'clock, and should they stand firm – simply go somewhere else. The key thing to know in the evening is the time for last orders: a restaurant that advertises its closure at 11.30 p.m. still might well refuse to take an order much after ten: no good rolling up at 11.25 and expecting the full three courses, because you're going to go hungry, chum.

See also: BOOKING, BRASSERIE

ORDERING

It is perfectly all right to take as long as you like in deciding what to order – just not to the point of driving your dining companions to the brink of despair. Announcing your dilemmas, chopping and changing, humming and hawing ... it really isn't that awfully amusing. If there is some term or bit of foreign gobbledegook on the menu that you don't understand (and restaurants derive enormous and impossible joy from ensuring that always there will be at the very least one of these), then don't guess: ask. Men in particular will be reluctant to do this as it endangers their carefully fostered image of omniscience (this misplaced vanity not unakin to their refusal ever to ask for directions). A decent waiter will be able to put you right – though more typically he will not understand so much as the nature of the question, nor possibly even the English language. If you do not require a starter, say so; there is no stigma whatsoever, and that goes also for ordering two starters, one in lieu of a main. Ask, too, if you are unsure as to whether the dish will require extra sides, or you are unclear as to the relative sizes of the starter and main portions of the same dish.

In the old days, it was quite usual for the host to ascertain the desires of each of his guests, remember the lot, and relay it to the waiter. This has rather fallen away, everyone tending now to order for themselves in turn. Either way, it should be made plain to the waiter which dish is for whom, and a good waiter in a good restaurant will remember – either because he is good at this, or, more likely, through a system of simple code on his order pad: because you do not at all want him holding aloft a selection of dishes and calling out, 'Who's the salmon ...?' and nor just plonking them down willy-nilly and leaving it to the diners to sort it all out. And talking of the order pad – do insist that it is used. Often you will be smugly assured by your waiter that they have no need of such a thing: ignore this. The smugger they are, the more sure they are to get the whole damn order around their necks.

If you are in a regular haunt, you will probably be eager to order exactly what you ordered last time (half the point of a regular haunt), and therefore will be anticipating your favourite with relish. If you are in an unfamiliar place, however, you might have been dithering just a bit – but when eventually the meals are served, do not be over concerned to find yourself suffering from a severe case of plate envy: wishing to goodness that you had ordered what the person next to you ordered because, oh my God … just *look* at it! Just so perfectly sublime – and particularly when contrasted against the dull and miserable offering that you now are expected to plough through. Any connoisseur of restaurant behaviour will tell you that this condition is quite normal – not to say incurable. Do not, however, actually voice this new and all-consuming lust … because if you are dining with someone scrupulously well-mannered, they will feel prompted to offer to swap, and never should someone be put into such a position. And no, of *course* you shouldn't agree to the swap – what are you *thinking* about?!

By way of a postscript, there ought to be added the following truism: if, when a waiter first comes along to take your order, you are not quite ready – still are teetering between this alternative and that – so therefore you request just one more minute finally to decide … said waiter will nod, smile broadly, slope away into darkness and then enter into a murderously terminal sulk – as a result of which you will not set eyes upon him again for a very, very long time.

See also: ETIQUETTE, MENUS, REGULAR HAUNTS, SERVICE

Abroad. That's where all of us were infected with a taste for dining *en plein air* … al fresco … beneath a canopy of stars. And by 'abroad', we largely are talking about the Mediterranean – with the inevitable and courteous nod in the direction of the ubiquitous American and Australian backyard 'barbies' – for it is in the South of France, on the Italian Riviera, a Greek island that we picture ourselves at our very leisured best: beneath the dappled shade of vines, olive or lemon grove, the gingham cloth askew upon the slightly rickety table, a huge and steaming bowl of something authentic to the area and impossibly delicious, piles of warm and downy just-picked peaches, much bright-green salad, buckets of something chilled and a cluster of good local reds, beautiful people, honey-tanned and in linen and Panamas, laughing indulgently – and nothing to do for the whole of the afternoon, and on into the twilit evening.

But in Blighty we do things differently, while stubbornly and very deludedly imagining it to be quite the same. Though of course we will worry incessantly about the weather – and rightly. We might think that a garden get-together or barbecue is a rather nice idea … but what if, on the day, it rains? Marquees are expensive – and a back-garden affair beneath a leaden sky as occasional droplets plop down merely to tease you wickedly is simply not to be borne. But we will persist with the thing, because eating outdoors is now our inalienable right, and a sign to all writ hugely in the bright, blue sky that 'Summer Is Finally Here!' So big and capable he-men will continue to don aprons bearing such slogans as 'Head Chef' or 'Come And Get It!' while they make the party nauseous with the reek of lighter fuel in their desperation to quickly bring the briquettes to their optimum heat. Then they can frazzle sausages that nonetheless will remain, within, a hotbed of pinkly raw bacteria, while committing every other sort of unspeakable culinary atrocity, these most often involving the sacrifice of perfectly blameless steaks.

Not everyone knows how to do a picnic as well as Edouard Manet. This famous painting of 1863, *Le Déjeuner sur l'herbe*, really ought to serve as an abiding lesson to all mankind, as well as an indication of the eternal truth that some of us feel the cold more than others.

Similarly the picnic. The picnic may safely be filed under the following truism: a positively brilliant idea ... which is how it should remain. Because we are rarely talking *Déjeuner sur l'herbe*, even if a chubby female of the party is inclined to get naked (and what with nettles, poison ivy and the omnipresent wasp, she'd have to be pretty far gone on the soupily warm Sancerre to contemplate any such thing). The picnic can be a lovely affair, though – but do keep it simple. You do not want a vast and spiffy wicker hamper with a full complement of bone china and crystal glassware, because apart from its inherent absurdity, even before you add the food and drink you will need a team of burly native bearers even to hoist the thing. Either get one of the many dedicated companies (from Fortnum & Mason downwards) to pack you a tempting selection in disposable packaging, or else stick to modest, easy-to-eat food (you don't need to be carving a chicken on a blanket) and gluggable wine that's fine at whatever temperature it happens to be (Beaujolais, say – and although screw tops are ideal, boxes and cans are very much not). Keep it to just a few amusing people, and as impromptu as the weather will permit. Do not park the car in a lay-by, set up a foldaway table and chairs, unpack the Thermos and be munching your egg-and-cress sandwiches while watching the lorries go by.

In cities – and particularly London, owing to its being a notorious 'melting pot of ethnic diversity' – there will be street food. This need not necessarily mean whatever discarded horror a vagrant might pick up off the pavement, this having been carelessly discarded by an irresponsible citizen, though it very easily might. More generally it translates as food that is 'good to go', as the imported phrase intensely annoyingly has it. So if you are in Chinatown, you pretty much will know what to expect (noodles 'r' us), as so you would in, say, Brick Lane (curries). Late-night kebabs or burgers from a van are obviously a no-no, but when next you canter towards one you will be drunk and ravenous and no word of caution from me or anyone else stands the slightest chance of stopping you. There are much finer vans around now, though – usually specializing in just the one thing, be it superior fish and chips, sausages or the classic English tea: these are generally pretty spiffy, and will run to the essential napkin. In the East End there are now things called Street Feasts – impromptu 'food raves', as they like them to be known – with all sorts of vans congregating seemingly within an instant, courtesy of Twitter (they call the messages 'tweats', I'm afraid). This, predictably, came out of New York and San Francisco, though in London I think it could be destined for even greater things.

And then there is outdoor eating at a restaurant. Which can – on the right day, in the ideal company, given the perfect balance of sunlight and shade, and at an establishment that very much knows what it is doing – be superb. But we do not want a table for two rammed on to a narrow pavement on a busy thoroughfare, do we? Even – or particularly – if the area is said to be 'vibrant'. Because it will be noisy and blowy and the food will go cold and have bits in it and people will gape at this novel and farcical addition to colourful street theatre (i.e. you) and then will jog you as they squeeze their way past, and the wine will just go everywhere: never be tempted. Gardens outside pubs can be a lot more spacious, but generally are choked with smokers, dogs and children, so that can be a worry too. You are really best off just inside an air-conditioned restaurant with a summery view – or else in your own back garden, which at least boasts the bonus of a very nearby house to duck into if it all becomes simply too awful. Because most often, it's better in than out.

See also: **CHILDREN, FOREIGN, SMOKING**

OVERHEADS

By which I mean those of the restaurant, not yours – because you, clearly, have decided that eating out is one of the overheads you are prepared to bear. But for a restaurant, the question is crucial and highly involved: if they get the costing wrong, overheads can quickly cripple a place, and ultimately bury it. People unused to eating out are often dismayed by the sight of the prices: 'How can they possibly justify thirty quid for *that*?!' Well, they don't have to justify it, of course: these are the advertised prices, quite out in the open, and if you think them exorbitant, you are perfectly free to dine somewhere else. But it is very naive and actually quite insulting to the restaurant to compare the price of a dish with the market cost of the primary ingredient. When you buy some steak in your local butcher, that, basically, is the total cost of the meal you are about to cook. You do not factor in such as butter, oil, seasoning … and what do a few potatoes and greens cost? Next to nothing. But a restaurant has no such luxury: they must take account of all of this. Which is no more than the teeniest tip of a totally daunting iceberg: decor, rent, business rates, insurance, staffing (huge in itself), laundry, cleaning, electricity, printing, flowers, promotion, breakages, wastage, technology, maintenance … probably a whole lot more – and this is before they have bought in so much as a stick of celery.

In the face of all this, it actually often amazes me how very *cheap* eating in a restaurant can be. Also, one must never forget: they are not there simply to serve you and cover their overheads – it is a business, and profit just has to be engendered. Which is why the sneaky incidentals are usually disproportionately pricey: wine, most obviously (mark-ups of 300 to 400 per cent are common), but also side dishes, a cover charge, service charge, extra sauces, bread, coffee, and so on. There is often much more money to be made on all of these than from the meals themselves.

So, having received the bill, please don't complain about the prices: you either choose to eat here, or you don't.

See also: BILL, COMPLAINING, TIPPING, VALUE, WINE LIST

PASS

In the best-run restaurants, a chef or sous-chef will call out 'Service!' (pronounced the French way) the moment a dish is ready to be taken away and served – whereupon the relevant waiter will be stationed right there and immediately do just that. But although the chef is presumably happy with his efforts, there really ought to be someone else in authority – the head chef, ideally – who also gives it the once-over at the pass: the final check in the quality control, which should be constant at every stage of the cooking in order to ensure that the diner will have no cause for complaint. That, anyway, is the theory – but how many times have I (and you) been presented with things that never should have progressed so far as the table, and often very obviously, too: overdone meat when rare was requested, a dangerously overflowing pool of gravy, a separated sauce, half-cooked pastry, unset jelly … all very evident to the diner at the very first glance, so why not the chef? This is a pretty clear sign of an overworked, understaffed and slapdash kitchen. Such places should learn from the classic Westerns: when dealing with a rogue, the only thing to do is head him off at the pass.

See also: PRESENTATION, SERVICE

PEOPLE

Hell is other people … right? Well, yes and no – because, as I think we all know rather too well, there are people and people … and glittering company in a restaurant can be very heaven. But of course that company has been selected by you; what, though, of all those people who just happen to be seated around you? What if they are intrusive? Or vilely mannered? Or just plain loud – because you will have noticed that the people possessed of the most hideous voices will not so much speak, as always declaim. As if they are magnanimously eager for everyone in the whole of the place to benefit from the joy of their every fabulous syllable – not to miss a single gem. It's a problem, but one that largely has to be swallowed … unless, of course, it becomes truly outrageous, by which time the management already should have nimbly but subtly stepped in. To request an alternative table far from the madding crowd should be a pointed and last resort – though if the head waiter or manager hadn't already seen this coming, then he is hardly worth his salt. People are wholly necessary to a restaurant – no one enjoys a meal in a deserted space – but politesse absolutely demands that each keeps to his own: do not foist your gaiety, jokes, ripe language or drunkenness on to others, as they should not foist it unto you.

See also: ETIQUETTE, SERVICE, TABLES

PIZZA

The humble nineteenth-century Neapolitan pizza has risen to conquer the world, leaving its indelible handprint just about everywhere. Which, when you think of it, is really quite an achievement for a circle of dough with a spattering of bits on. The really good ones these days – although people will always argue whether 'really good' comes down to a soft or crispy base – will be made in a proper, wood-fired pizza oven, usually imported from Italy. These vast kilns, however, very much require someone who knows what they are doing: sometimes, a pizzeria will have all the top equipment, but lack a bloke who understands that just seconds too long in the furnace and what you have on your hands is something that is no longer eatable. Because people who tell you that they actually like the black and burned bits are lying.

Most pizzas probably come in the form of takeaways, or else are delivered in a dubious state on the back of a moped. Food that is freshly and quickly prepared frankly doesn't travel – and that is true even if they get your address right the first time and do not take your delivery to a street with a vaguely similar name in an entirely different borough; and when the pizza finally does arrive, often after several increasingly irate phone calls, even the carton seems to have given up the ghost and quietly expired, so God alone knows what the margarita can be like. We were seduced for decades by American films featuring the pizza-delivery boy: we marvelled at how the boxes could be the size of a billiard table, and also at how extraordinarily frequently the pizza-delivery boy at the door turned out not to be the pizza-delivery boy at the door because one person inside the house would say, 'Did you order pizza?' and someone else would say, 'I didn't order pizza – didn't you order pizza?' and it quickly transpires that no one in fact has ordered pizza but they open the door anyway and sure enough it turns out that the pizza-delivery boy is not actually the pizza-delivery boy but a Mafia hit man with a sub-machine gun and everyone gets blown away and their dying thoughts, who could say, are maybe centred around wishing that, in the light of the fact that no one actually had ordered any pizza, they hadn't in fact opened the bloody door – and possibly even wishing that someone had ordered some pizza, because then the whole evening might have turned out rather nicer.

See also: ITALIAN, TAKEAWAY

PLAT DU JOUR

A proper *plat du jour* can truly be a lovesome thing, and often most assuredly the direction to take – the chief ingredient dictated by the season and market availability, ideally – and probably a bargain, into the bargain. The thing you have to guard against is its actually being a *plat du hier*, as it were: the stuff that's been hanging around for maybe ages that still is being dickied up as a well-priced dish-of-the-day in the hope that finally the restaurant may be shot of it. If you know the restaurant, there should be no anxiety at all – otherwise, just ask: you'll probably receive a truthful answer. Some restaurants will simultaneously be offering 'specials', a set lunch and a *prix fixe* menu to boot, which is not just rather confusing but also can be something of a worry – because it can't *all* be freshly laid on for just that day, can it, really? Ask questions, and feel your way.

See also: BARGAIN LUNCH, MENUS, SERVICE

POP-UPS

A fairly recent addition to the urban restaurant scene, and often a seductive novelty. A pop-up is something that appears quite suddenly and seemingly out of nowhere in a variety of unlikely settings (I have encountered them everywhere from a disused warehouse to a ball-room in Claridge's, by way of Selfridges' rooftop and the basement of a pornographic bookshop), and can be peddling anything from fashionable street food to very grande cuisine indeed, courtesy of a household-name star chef. In such cases as this, the pop-up will come in the shape of a perfectly formed cameo set amid the cacophonous bling of London (and pretty much certainly, it will be London) for a strictly prescribed period ... and so by the time you've heard of it, the place is booked solid. Or it can be a youthful, ambitious partner-ship temporarily taking over the fag-end of an unexpired lease of something or other, and that will determine the restaurant's longevity. There is always a word-of-mouth, blog-driven buzz and urgency sur-rounding any new pop-up venture, the intimation being that if you don't get your skates on pronto, it will have been and gone and then you will have *missed* it. And if there is one thing upon this earth that the fashionable diner-about-town can simply not so much as even contemplate, let alone bear, it is *missing* something ...

See also: BUZZ, FASHION, STAR CHEF, YOUNG PLACES

PRESENTATION

Many restaurants – and certainly all of those that practise or aspire to 'fine dining' – will spend an inordinate amount of time and care on the presentation of not just the table, but also each individual dish and flourish. The grandest (and, admittedly, very often quite hilarious) flourish of them all being the synchronized removal of the great silver domes covering the diners' dishes: ta-dah! The less embarrassable waiters all seem to enjoy the theatrical nonsense of it, while the maître d' – whose carefully timed raising of the eyebrow they so eagerly anticipate – positively revels in the entire display. All you have to remember is not to smirk openly – and nor should you make any sudden movement at the crucial denouement, or else as the great and gleaming things are summarily whisked away, you might so very easily get clonked around the side of the head.

It goes without saying that prior to your arrival, every single detail will have been scrutinized: the waiters' uniforms, the napery, the flowers, the stemware, the intricately folded napkins … and the large, impressive charger set at each place and probably bearing the insignia of the restaurant, whose only function ever is to be instantly removed before your very eyes. It will be replaced with a plate of quite a different order, upon which will be set a second plate – with possibly a doily between the two – this one conceivably actually bearing some food, though by no means necessarily: it might take yet a third before that finally is permitted to happen. There are fashions that come and go when it comes to the presentation of the dish itself: colourful dribbles, droplets and lunatic swishes of this and that seem to be here to stay (how else to apparently fill those gargantuan white dishes?), though the practice of erecting towers of food, these to culminate in something spun, ornate and inedible, does seem finally to be on the wane. It does always appear just slightly perverse of a chef to painstakingly construct a narrow and rickety pile of all the meal's constituents, this obliging the diner in the very first instance to take

Three very proud and capable sous-chefs at New York's
Ritz-Carlton in the 1940s, earnestly displaying their peerless
creations to the tallest photographer in the history of the world.

it all apart again so that it may be nicely laid out, and then eaten. Similarly, the modish idea of 'deconstruction' does appear just as perverse: something or other that is pretty famous for being of a piece – cottage pie, say, or a fruit flan – will have its filling divorced from its top, the two arranged side by side. Well, okay ... but why? Another fad of the moment is the porringer made up of minuscule scooped indentation and colossal rim, this ensuring that the spoonful's journey twixt soup and lip is a lengthy and worrying one.

All of this is at the top end, of course. And while the majority of restaurants will continue simply to put in front of you a plate of food, just as always they have done, there is a growingly assertive rump of fashionable places that have embraced wholeheartedly the anti-art of non-presentation. So ... the table will be bare, the cutlery not laid out in the customary pattern but dumped on top of a paper napkin, or else just slung into an enamel bucket for you to fish out for yourself. Shop-bought sauces will be pushily present in their stickily congealing shop-bought bottles – and never mind chargers, saucers and doilies, matey: the food will arrive on anything you can imagine, but never anything so irredeemably stupid as a plate. Chunks of greasy timber, slices of slate, slabs of marble, panes of glass ... it's all good, so long as it is rimless, and therefore may be guaranteed to ensure that bits of grub and gravy will trickle all over the table (and if ice cream is involved, the race is on to get it down you before it melts and runs away just everywhere). This punk approach – the return to the caveman ideal – is particularly appreciated by the young, to whom primitivism comes so very naturally.

See also: DECOR, FASHION, FINE DINING, SERVICE, TABLES, YOUNG PLACES

PRIZE DINNERS

The best thing you can hope for, if ever you find yourself having to attend a prize dinner, is that you are not one of the blighted and unfortunate buggers who are actually up for the prize. Because yes, okay – it's lovely if you win, of course it is, but look at it: the odds are stacked against you, aren't they? There could well be six or more of you, sweating away there; and while all the blissfully uninvolved guests and hangers-on can airily dabble in the prawny thing, pick at the chickeny thing, toy with the vodka-jelly thing – while concentrating hard upon becoming really quite gloriously smashed on the corporate and endless booze – you of course have no appetite whatsoever and are barely daring to drink at all because although you know in your waters that you haven't got a swine's chance in bloody hell of winning this goddam sodding, sodding prize, still you are fingering clammily this overlong and frankly awful speech that nonetheless you felt obliged to cobble up … and people to either side will insist on addressing their comments to you, almost as if they imagine you to be listening, or something. And after, when all the shouting's done, either you are borne up on high, literally or metaphorically – or else (rather more likely, let's face it, chum) you are in receipt of one or two consolatory slaps on the back (before these people rapidly retreat, because nobody loves a loser), but finally determined to get seriously into the corporate and endless booze, the speech in pieces and scattered on the floor. The good news being that you missed absolutely nothing in having foregone fooling with the prawny thing, the chickeny thing, the vodka-jelly thing …

See also: **CHARITY DINNERS, CORPORATE ENTERTAINING, FORMAL DINNERS**

PUDDING

Dessert: it's a word you see on menus, but maybe do not feel altogether happy about using any more. And nobody, one trusts, any longer says 'afters' ... 'sweet' has long ago succumbed to being buried beneath a cackling landslide of ridicule ... and so we are left with 'pudding': an amply pleasing, well-upholstered, thoroughly English and even Falstaffian sort of a word – and so pudding it is. Ignore all the foreigners who laugh at our referring to such as a soufflé, mille-feuille or even ice cream as 'pudding', and ignore too their continuing to laugh at our being confronted with a steaming spotted dick with custard (pudding if ever there was one) and then actually eating it. They know no better: they scoff when they would be far better off – and you know what I mean – simply scoffing.

In Britain, of course, a certain 'naughtiness' surrounds the concept of pudding – as it does with jam and cream-covered scones at teatime, or chocolates at any time at all. Sweet and gorgeous confections are seen to be not so much married bliss, as the slap-and-tickle that makes the gastronomic world go round: how's-your-father, a touch of nooky, something on the side ... when the meat and two veg are done with, well now here comes a bit of the other. Carry On Pudding. This attitude is ingrained, it is never going to go away, and so we might as well embrace it – and if it serves to make pudding all the more of a treat, well then so much the better.

The dessert trolley is sometimes seen to be the devil's own chariot – and the devil has a smooth line in seduction. So a woman might stare lasciviously at the dazzle of coloured and creamy delights and decide she wants to eat the *lot* ... but will, with sighing reluctance, decline so much as even a taste. 'I mustn't', she will say. On a diet, perhaps, or simply not wishing to appear gluttonous (and this is especially true in the company of slimmer, younger women). A little gentle pressure is in order, but only just a little: if she weakens to the point of saying, 'I shouldn't ...' then she's almost certainly up for a crème brûlée. For other women, pudding is the *raison d'être* of any meal, pure and simple – all fish-and-meaty preamble no more than mere conversation. Men, wouldn't you know, approach the whole thing from a different perspective: often, pudding is perceived to be 'unmanly'. Cheese is preferable – particularly the strong and odorous varieties, a savoury such as Welsh rarebit being even better – but pastel-coloured gooey things …? No – they smack too much of the nursery, or else are redolent of scented and lacy underpinnings. It is all right to like chocolate, though: chocolate is emergency rations. And *real* puddings, such as the aforementioned spotted dick, sponge pudding, treacle pudding, bread-and-butter pudding, Christmas pudding … these are mother's milk.

If you are in the sort of top-rate place that employs its own esteemed in-house patissier, you would be a fool to forego the genius's art: here will be the pastry of the gods. That said, 'home-made' is not the same thing at all, and by no means a guarantee of quality: there are many independent suppliers to the trade of cakes, trifles, flans and ice cream who are a great deal better at it than some well-meaning dope in the kitchen armed with no more than a recipe, optimism and a wooden spoon. Freshness, however, is always key – be it gateau, fruit salad or tart. And talking of tarts … Please: do not order tarte Tatin unless you are in a place that not only will cook it to order (twenty minutes, normally), but also knows and understands precisely what it is they are meant to be cooking. For the sins that daily are committed in the name of tarte Tatin are both legion and appalling.

See also: CHEESE, TEA

QUALITY

We all know that quality is key: no one recommends with enthusiasm this really charming little restaurant where the staff are quite delightful, the prices unbelievably low and the quality of the food just bloody disgusting. But one's expectations of quality must always be realistic. If you book in to a three-star Michelin restaurant, you are perfectly entitled to expect (and are paying through the nose for) the very highest quality in every single aspect of the dining experience. It does not follow, of course, that any lesser restaurant that fails to deliver quality on so exalted a level is therefore a write-off: the anticipated quality must be commensurate with the ambition and price level of the establishment concerned. If you are in search of the perfect burger, you instinctively feel that you may not get it from a beaten-up van parked outside a dog track – though nor necessarily must you go to a top-flight West End brasserie. Quality in the middling places is something you really have to discover over time, but price must always come into it: if you are unwilling to spend more than a fiver on your meal, then obviously you cannot expect (and you sure as hell are not going to get) anything approaching the finest quality. But at a good greasy spoon or cafe, you might enjoy a top-quality breakfast for not much more … or else, for similar money, something quite repellent. Trial and error, then – and one of the reasons why, when we do find somewhere that meets our criteria, we tend quite wisely to stick with it.

In terms of quality, here is what always you are in search of: the common thing, done uncommonly well.

See also: BILL, BRASSERIE, CAFES, GREASY SPOONS, REGULAR HAUNTS, RESTAURANT GUIDES, STAR CHEFS, VALUE

QUEUING

Really? Truly? Not having me on …? But what on earth are you queuing for? No, honestly: I really can't imagine – it's just totally beyond me. Aren't there any other restaurants in town then, that you are forced to join a conga line outside this particular one? Are they giving away the food and drink tonight? Is that it? Is that why you are queuing? No – it's not, is it? It's simply because here is a fashionable new place; that's the truth – you might as well admit it. It's got the buzz. Everyone's talking about it. It's been trending all day long. And – the masterstroke, the clincher – they don't take bookings! But wouldn't you feel just very slightly ridiculous if I told you that inside this so very cool new pit there are in fact just tables galore? That the seemingly desperate and insatiable demand for them is carefully crafted and deliberately artificial? And that by queuing you are doing the proprietor an extraordinary favour by forming part of a free and living advertisement for the place – the sort that money cannot buy – this proclaiming to the entire neighbourhood that the restaurant is just so unspeakably fantastic that a long string of idiots (sorry: no offence – what I meant was, this collection of discerning and on-trend would-be diners) are willing to stand for hours in the freezing street? And further, that the existence of the queue duly gets reported in the press, goes viral on social media, all this underlining in red the extreme desirability of a table within this holy of holies?

Well, now you do know all that, grow up, for goodness' sake: amble into a restaurant that is pleased to see you, where you will be ushered with a smile and straight away to a comfortable table. And that place you were queuing for? Probably no good. In a few months, you won't even remember its name, the queue having moved on to some other newly popped-up hellhole: it'll be shut before the year is out.

See also: BOOKING, BUZZ, FASHION, POP-UPS, YOUNG PLACES

QUOTATIONS

Hardly strictly relevant to the thrust and nature of the book – but, I hope you will agree, an amusing diversion nonetheless: a small selection of associated quotations.

'It's easier to be faithful to a restaurant than it is to a woman.'
FEDERICO FELLINI

'I was eating in a Chinese restaurant downtown.
There was a dish called Mother & Child Reunion. It's chicken and eggs. And I said, "I gotta use that one."'
PAUL SIMON

'There are advantages to being a star – you can always get a table in a full restaurant.'
INGRID BERGMAN

'Memories are like mulligatawny soup in a cheap restaurant.
It is best not to stir them.'
P. G. WODEHOUSE

'In Tulsa, restaurants have signs that say "Sorry, We're Open".'
ROSEANNE BARR

'The finest landscape in the world is improved by a good inn in the foreground.'
SAMUEL JOHNSON

'Great restaurants are, of course, nothing but mouth-brothels. There is no point in going to them if one intends to keep one's belt buckled.'
FREDERIC RAPHAEL

'Vegetarians, and their Hezbollah-like splinter faction, the vegans, are a persistent irritant to any chef worth a damn … the enemy of everything good and decent in the human spirit.'
ANTHONY BOURDAIN

'If you're choking to death in a restaurant, you can just say the magic words "Heimlich manoeuvre". Trouble is, it's difficult to say "Heimlich manoeuvre" when you're choking to death.'
EDDIE IZZARD

'A tumbler tells me that a person doesn't appreciate wine, and it is going to be second rate – I might be a bit of a snob, but I'd rather not drink plonk.'
MICHEL ROUX JR

'In pubs, at least, food is the curse of the drinking classes.'
KINGSLEY AMIS

'No one really likes restaurant work.'
FERRAN ADRIÀ

'The only time to eat diet food is while you're waiting for the steak to cook.'
JULIA CHILD

'Chefs are nutters. They're all self-obsessed, delicate, dainty, insecure little souls and absolute psychopaths. Every last one of them.'
GORDON RAMSAY

'A gourmet who thinks of calories is like a tart who looks at her watch.'
JAMES BEARD

'Let us eat and drink, for tomorrow we shall die.'
ISAIAH 22: 13

REGULAR HAUNTS

They're just wonderful, aren't they? Those three or four places (if you're very damned lucky) that you always can depend upon, like a pair of softly worn-in slippers, or an amatory Golden Labrador. Restaurants become regulars for any number of disparate reasons: a club, maybe, where you have to make no formal arrangements to meet anyone, but are confident that in the bar and subsequently at table there will always be one or more people with whom you enjoy spending time (and if there isn't, of course, then you are a member of quite the wrong club). Or if the restaurant is truly local: you can't be bothered to cook tonight, so why not amble around the corner to that trusty little Italian where you know you'll be welcome, the food will be decent, and the bill won't break you? Or it's handy for work. Or it's the place you stumbled upon countless years ago and still you meet up there with the same old crew every couple of months or so: because why go to the trouble of uprooting yourselves and finding somewhere different?

Few would ever cite their regular haunts as the greatest restaurants in the universe – and often it's hardly to do with the food at all. And this is where the restaurant itself has to play its essential part – and certainly if those loyal and enthusiastic regulars are to be retained (because to a restaurateur, dependable return visits ought to be the ultimate goal). So: if a regular favours the table in the alcove just to the left of the window, the restaurant must always strive to give it to him. In turn, of course, the punter must give reasonable notice: you can't just turn up entirely unannounced and expect to have the run of the place. It goes without saying that the welcome will be warm – and one hopes and trusts that the warmth is genuine. One curious thing about regular haunts is that the regular haunters tend to want their meals and drinks to be similarly constant: it's not at all unusual for the same dishes to be ordered time after time, along with a bottle of the usual. So for the restaurant to have that bottle at the ready is a thoughtful and always appreciated touch, as is the occasional drink on the house (and certainly at Christmas). The staff should be friendly, of course – and in an Italian, Spanish or Greek place a certain amount of hugging just has to be anticipated … but this must never extend to back-slapping, rib-nudging nor joining you at the table for a drink (unless possibly the proprietor, who has been expressly invited so to do).

One unexplained phenomenon is how a place can be a regular for years, and through no fault of the management, change in the menu or embarrassment at your own behaviour, you suddenly realize that you haven't been there for simply ages: the sands have shifted, and it has fallen off your radar. This can happen, and the schism tends to be permanent. It's rather like personal relationships: the more exten-ded the gap, the less conceivable it increasingly seems even to think of bridging it – because the last thing you need is to be met with a row of doleful faces and a plangent, not to say accusatory, enquiry as to where on earth you have *been* … But it's all quite okay, because by that time you will happily have established yourself as a regular some-where else entirely.

See also: **BOOKING, CLUBS, ETIQUETTE, FRONT OF HOUSE, MENUS, SERVICE, SQUEEZED MIDDLE, TABLES, VALUE**

RESTAURANT GUIDES

There was a chilly time – back in the days that foodies could do worse than refer to as the Dark Ages – when, as our torch-bearing and trailblazing pioneering advisers, we had but Raymond Postgate's *Good Food Guide* and that of the eternally blessed Egon Ronay to light our way. But then, there were pitifully few restaurants for us to be guided through: in the early guides, the classifications could be broadly divided into 'Posh, Expensive and Ultimately Disappointing Hotel', 'Authentic Greasy Spoon', 'Trusty Little Italian' and 'Dire'. Well, the *Good Food Guide* still is with us, along with quite a few more of varying reputation. The most talked about, however, remains Michelin ... and although for a long time there have been dark, disgruntled murmurings about how – in this bright new egalitarian day and age (ho ho) – the guide is increasingly irrelevant, the bestowal of one-to-three glittering stars patronizing, autocratic and out of step with the modern attitude to dining out, the most vociferous gainsayers tending to be restaurateurs who have failed to be awarded one. I think that Michelin still is rather important, if only as a reasonably unwavering benchmark – though of course, we mustn't follow it too slavishly, nor ever assume that an establishment excluded from its attention is therefore beneath our consideration.

Over the last five or more years, the Michelin guide has opened up to a surprising degree, doling out stars (or one, anyway) to establishments to which they never before would have deigned. The guide also advises upon and recommends very many lesser eateries and pubs, but of course it is the bona fide Michelin stars that still are most highly regarded. The better restaurants remain in thrall to them, whatever their proprietors may say: they establish the chef among his respected peers, ensure attention from his (or her, increasingly) contemporaries abroad (as well as the gourmet tourists) and enable the restaurant to hoick up its prices overnight, and maybe even for the very first time experience the bittersweet joy of turning away requests for tables due to being fully booked for the foreseeable future. Michelin employs inspectors who really are true pros, and always anonymous ... and this cannot be said for such guides as Harden's, say. This is an annual distilled compilation of the views and experiences of eager amateurs: unpaid, settling their own bill (and you do honestly wonder how they can be bothered), but still very much open to other influences – such as the chef/proprietor of a raved-about restaurant being the said raver's wife. For similar reasons, online guides should be viewed with care. Whereas the best guides can often be the opinions of people whose tastes and inclinations you both share and respect, most influence these days will stem from individual reviews in newspapers and magazines ... and now, so very conveniently, you can read about those – in Restaurant Reviews.

See also: BUZZ, DECOR, FASHION, PRESENTATION, RESTAURANT REVIEWS, SERVICE, STAR CHEFS, WORLD'S 50 BEST RESTAURANTS

RESTAURANT REVIEWS

Everyone these days is a restaurant critic, or believes they ought to be – because look: it's the best and easiest job in the universe, right? Well, yes and no: no one is comparing the task of eating out in different restaurants every week with the rigours of coal mining, but the better critics do make it seem to be rather more of a pushover than is necessarily the case. To declare an interest, for the past five years I have written a weekly restaurant review for a small but highly influential London newspaper (well, since you press me on the matter, it is the *Hampstead & Highgate Express* – or *Ham & High*, to its chums), so I've gradually learnt just a little of this. But because nothing is more enjoyable to read than an absolutely gory and gleeful trashing of a restaurant, where the disgruntled or outraged critic is truly gnashing and letting rip, people might imagine that the reviewer carefully combs through the available restaurants in urgent search of somewhere that is likely to be lamentable so that he can dip his metaphorical nib into the viscous cliché of vitriol and generally wallow in having himself a field day. I have never known this to be the case. Every reviewer of my acquaintance (and it's a small world) is after the same thing as everyone else: if not excellence (always favourite), then at least a good meal, well served, and in pleasant surroundings. So it is genuinely surprising in this highly competitive and cut-throat foodie world how often one does discover a place that is truly bad, or else so utterly mediocre that one is forced to wonder about its future.

The thing is: you have to trust your reviewer – and your faith will ultimately depend upon whether he or she is going about the business in the proper and above-board manner: booking under a pseudonym (if famous), never announcing that a review is to be written, and never accepting free meals. These days, such professional practice is generally confined to the national press and the more upmarket glossies (as well as, I might add, the *Ham & High*). Most other things you will read are paid-for listings, or might be termed an 'advertorial', or some other weasel word: all of these come down to collusion. The restaurant has offered some hack and attendant floozy a buckshee meal with booze in frank exchange for a highly adulatory 'review'. You know them when you see them: they are relentlessly upbeat while reading like a very poor school essay, and generally will close with the determinedly joyous declaration, 'I'll be back!' (which, actually, they won't – because next time they'll be expected to pay, you see, so instead they'll freeload somewhere else and file the identical fawning and idiotic copy, changing only the name of the restaurant). Dismiss these. And dismiss also the bulk of what you will read online: here are either family and friends being nice, or those with a bone to pick and corporate rivals being nasty.

If you read a reviewer regularly, you will come to know his tastes, enthusiasms and prejudices (because they all have them). If these coincide with your own, you're home and dry – for you will always know to take that reviewer's advice as to whether to go to or avoid any given restaurant. A good review, of course, will impart far more than the quality of the food: as you will see from this A–Z, there is a great deal more to eating out than that. And humour is pretty much essential – because all we are ultimately talking about, amid the hubris, is a plate of food and a jolly time. But do remember this: a critic does not ever 'give' a good or a bad review, the restaurant earns it.

See also: RESTAURANT GUIDES, WORLD'S 50 BEST RESTAURANTS

RETRO

It used to be easy to pinpoint the little retro niche, but increasingly – due wholly, I suspect, to popular demand – it has been seeping into the mainstream, if not actually threatening to take it over wholesale. I suppose it all began with the nostalgic recreation of the American diner, which we had never actually experienced at first hand, but nonetheless had thrilled to in just how many vintage films? The nursery pastels and ritzy chrome, the neon, the white-piped red leather-ette swivel stools and booths, the individual table jukeboxes (which never actually worked – it was going to be 1950s doo-wop, whatever button you pressed) and those little straw and napkin dispensers. Somewhere would redly glow a Coca-Cola sign, and if you were truly blessed, the waitress would be pretty, red-lipsticked, gingham-skirted, white-aproned … and in order to take your order (cheeseburger loaded, natch) would whip out a pencil from behind her ear. So far, so Yankee. Then British retro began to creep in: mismatched Utility furniture, nippy-style waitresses (mob caps were always good) … but really it was more to do with the food: hearty pies, toad-in-the-hole, Lancashire hot-pot, Irish stew, Sunday roasts (yes of course with Yorkshire pudding) and things like rice pudding, Eton mess and spotted dick. Also prawn cocktail. And Black Forest gateau.

There is actually a very good reason why these dishes and many more of a similar ilk will simply not lay down and die: after the initial enthusiasm inevitably come the years of embarrassed ridicule … but then they will always rise again – because people love to eat them. And I am all for people eating what they love. As to the French and Austrian brasseries and cafes … here is retro that never actually went away in the first place. The same is true of the fish-and-chip shop and the greasy spoon: God bless them, every one.

See also: BURGERS, DECOR, FISH, GREASY SPOONS, SUNDAY ROAST

ROMANCE

Cooking at home for your special squeeze: that is surely a romantic thing to do, no? And particularly if you are a man – but only, let me underline, if you are good at it (because cooking badly is not sexy, though doing anything badly is not sexy, and that includes sex). And so although it remains a self-evident truism that romance in all its incarnations is best conducted behind closed doors, the majority of food guides still will persist in devoting a section to 'romantic restaurants' – and if ever you were groping for a prime example of proffering a poisoned chalice while sticking your neck out just about as far as it will go, then here you have it, in all its crushed velvet-cushioned and candlelit splendour. People will always hold wildly differing views about quite what constitutes 'romantic', and we call these people men and women. Though of course if a couple is truly in love, the most romantic restaurant is simply any restaurant of any description in the whole wide world – or, failing that, no restaurant at all. But otherwise, trouble looms in the form of the terrible touchstones of 'romance', the trite and predictable tropes of it all, which have become so indelibly ingrained that both restaurant and diners now just dumbly enact their roles, strutting and fretting, within this flagrant theatre of the absurd, and without ever remotely thinking about it.

The man automatically will go for somewhere with low ceilings and lighting, pink tablecloths, sweet flowers, glowing candles … he might think to pre-order some chilled pretty rosé or champagne … he may even think it a good thing should there be on hand some farcically got-up guitarist, eager to render a serenade … or even some boot-faced gypsy woman hanging about who will threaten to saddle him with a single red rose within a cellophane tube ('for da booty-foo lie-dee') in exchange for little more than the cost of a dozen from M&S. Certain restaurants will lay all this on because they imagine it is expected of them (for it hardly would occur to them that it also will

Pudding time. This charming nineteenth-century
French lithograph illustrates perfectly just what a booth was created for,
with both of the diners seemingly delighted with it all – while the waiter
falls prey to a sad contemplation of life, the universe and everything.

generate a fair whack of dosh). And women ... oh, the poor women, they just have to pretend to thrill to the entire scenario because it is famously supposed to be just what women will thrill to – and they are unhappily conscious, too, of all the expense their well-meaning yet ultimately benighted sap of a man has been put to, money which (if the couple are merely friends) she might well think could have been better put to that new pair of shoes she has had her eye on, or (if married) towards the looming cost of lagging the loft.

If you really utterly have to go through all this sort of thing, try to be guided by this: make sure that your table is well away from any other, because it's going to be embarrassing enough as it is. Do not order overtly 'sexy' food: oysters, asparagus and anything else involving fingers. Do not stick spoons in each other's mouths. Do not drink too much: it isn't romantic, and in this place will cost you an absolute fortune. Try not to propose: the diamond ring will catch the light and everyone will look, and if she is forced to tentatively and tenderly explain either that this is all so sudden and unexpected and she will need more time before she gives you her answer, or else that yes she loves you, but just not in *that* way ... then you will be compelled to kill yourself in public. Because one dreamy lover's romantic restaurant is a thwarted suitor's hellhole. And it surely goes without saying that you must on no account be there on Valentine's Day: are you *mad* ...?

And when you have reached the end of your 'romantic' lunch or dinner date in a restaurant, you must remember this: a kiss ain't just a kiss.

See also: DECOR, EXCUSE FINGERS, VALENTINE'S DAY

SAUCES

The only differentiation really to get straight about sauces is whether they are integral to the dish (as in pasta, blanquettes, flambés and so on) or simply form an accompaniment on the side. In these cases – Béarnaise, hollandaise, peppercorn, so many others – one may of course opt out of them altogether, or else request an alternative to the one suggested. If your choice is listed in the context of another dish on the menu, then obviously this should not present a problem. Otherwise, it is up to the restaurant whether they are prepared to knock you up such a thing (a decent place will) – but do ascertain that it isn't going to take an absolute age, or else there is a danger that your food is going to be hanging about, waiting for the sauce to catch up. With such a dish as fishcakes, ideally the sauce ought to be offered separately – preferably in the pan in which it was cooked – whereupon you can decide whether you want it to be ladled over or around the lovely golden things. As to bottled sauces … well, if you are in a burger place, you very much want and expect Heinz ketchup to be proudly present (along with Hellman's mayonnaise and French's mustard), while no self-respecting greasy spoon would be caught dead without HP. If, however, you spot a selection of these elsewhere (along with Sarson's vinegar anywhere but a chippy) you must – and quickly – ask yourself whether inadvertently you have wandered into quite the wrong place.

See also: BURGERS, GREASY SPOONS, OFF MENU, SERVICE

SEASONAL FOOD

Many diners – and most supermarket shoppers – can easily forget that there are any more such things as seasons for food. Luscious soft fruits and berries are always piled high in glorious coloured mountains, and such as turkey is by no means available only at Christmas. But it is so worthwhile to take greedy advantage of certain delicacies when they are naturally at their peak, and preferably native, while eschewing those that have been aggressively forced in massive bulk in some vast foreign hothouse, and then transported halfway across the globe. New-season English lamb, English asparagus and Jersey Royals spring eagerly to mind, effortlessly combining to form a perfect plateful – tantalizingly brief spring seasons for all of them, and you may be indulgently forgiven for ordering them every single day that they are available. Many will droolingly await August, so that they can savour the first of the grouse – and of course opinions differ as to whether it is a sacrilegious nonsense to wolf them down on the Glorious Twelfth itself (such indecent haste being rather redolent of the old, and now quite rightly discredited, Beaujolais Nouveau Race) … while others might demur at the practice of hanging them for so long that they become decidedly whiffy, not to say just this side of putrid. Personal taste, as with everything – my own preference being to eat them after two to four weeks of their having been peppered with shot (plain roasted, and of course with bread sauce, game chips and a not too bloody gravy). Most game does actually freeze very well, so do not necessarily dismiss it if it appears on a menu out of season: as ever, it helps if you know the restaurant and trust the kitchen. The old "'r' in the month' caveat about oysters has rather diminished in power, as now they are farmed in all sorts of unlikely places all the year round … but still there is nothing to beat natives, in season. It is good that occasionally Mother Nature is coquettishly sparing in her favours: it encourages us to be lusty, and relish them all the more.

See also: MENUS

SELF-SERVICE

Some people, I am told, are vigorously in favour of this concept: they say it is quick; they say it involves no fuss. But listen: what's the hurry? You're eating out, aren't you? And always that should be a pleasant and leisurely thing to do. As to fuss ... well, a little bit of the right sort of fuss can be a rather good thing: and we call that service. Half a century or more ago, self-service was a novelty. It was 'modern' – better still, it was 'contemporary', and therefore most passionately to be wished for. And so in a strip-lit, Formica-clad and Marley-tiled vacuum, people would queue, slide a Bakelite tray along a ridged aluminium shelf, gape at pre-prepared nothings through acrylic doors, select this and that, add a cellophaned briquette of fruitcake as a very special treat, decide between a whoosh of tea, churned-up milk that is masquerading as a bubbly milkshake but turns out disappointingly not to be, or else a warm bottle of cold drink, and finally – when the very bored woman on the till is done with her hasty totting-up – be astounded by what this sad little motley of bits and bobs can actually be costing, and so battle the way back through an irate and jostled line of grazers in order to replace the extortionately priced cellophaned briquette of fruitcake. But these days, surely people want no truck with any of all that sort of thing – unless, I suppose, in a fast-food chain ... but what on earth do you imagine you are doing in one of those? To me, the idea of self-service is on a par with self-table-setting, self-cooking and self-washing-up: I can get all that at home.

See also: CHAINS, FAST FOOD, SERVICE

SERVICE

You might think that when it comes to eating out, the quality of service is second only to that of the food ... but there are many who actually will place it at the very top of the list. That is not to say that the fodder is of no consequence – of course not – but while the consummation much to be wished for always must be the very best of both, there are many habitual diners who are more than happy to return time and time again to a restaurant where the food is not much more than perfectly okay for the money, while the welcome, front of house and service are just bang on and second to none. Few, however, will be content with sullen faces and inept, offhand and untrained waiters flinging food at you, no matter how fantastic the kitchen – because so often it is the entire experience of any particular lunch or dinner from entry to departure that will linger on and be talked about, long after the memory of what you actually ate is lost to the mists of time.

So what is good service? Well – you know it when you see it, of course, but let us get out of the way all that it decidedly isn't: and it isn't fawning, for a start. There are people, I'm afraid, who patronize only the very newest, most hyped and ruinously expensive restaurants (in fact, the more overtly overpriced the better) and come to view the entire establishment as their temporarily rented fiefdom, the staff no more than minions, merely there in order to flatter, grovel and stoically absorb every barely veiled slight or open rudeness that surely will be coming their way. The waiters in such establishments will have been instructed to swallow hard and go along with all of this: it will be explained to them that such arrogant punters as these are fundamental to the business and regard the right to be abusive as being included in the extortionate bill – and I simply cannot tell you how visibly demeaning all of this is for both the unfortunate staff and the vainglorious diner alike (though while the waiter will feel it deeply, the gaudy instigator most assuredly will not). This sort of 'service' is actually a disservice to manners, not to say the human condition. And so … from that extreme to the other: service should not be resented. In France, waiting at table is seen to be an honourable profession, often passed down from father to son (and particularly in the case of sommeliers): each one of them is rightly proud to be a vital part of the dining process. It is not always necessary to be quite so dedicated as that – but if a waiter simply loathes the idea of bringing food to a table, there to be consumed by someone else who possibly is richer than he and enjoys a far better lifestyle and so makes the waiter experience a bubbling urge to slaughter him with a cleaver … then he simply must pursue an alternative occupation: he might consider becoming a traffic warden, or maybe working for US Immigration, in both of which disciplines flagrant contempt is actively encouraged.

Nor should service be chummy. Friendly, yes – amiability encourages smiling, and smiling is essential. But not jokey, not larky, not pushy, not rib-nudging, and definitely not back-slapping: the waiter must remember that no matter how frequent and familiar, these paying customers are not his mates; he must simply contrive at all times to be professional, though affable. And of course, service must never, ever descend into rudeness: if a diner keeps on chopping and changing with his order, finally and at length deciding once and for all – and as soon as the waiter has written this down beneath all the crossings out says no, hang on, I'm not actually having that, I'm going to choose something else entirely … then the waiter, whatever might be grimly churning in the murkiest canyons of his mind, must not roar at him, 'Look, you stupid sod – just make up your bloody mind, can't you?!' Nor must he slap him with his notebook.

Another thing a waiter mustn't ever do is interrupt the conversation – and especially when one of the party is excitedly leading into the doubtless quite killing denouement of a truly hilarious story … and this is particularly the case if all the waiter has to say is, 'Is everything all right?' He may just about be permitted to say this once, and only once, at some slack point of the meal – but every waiter should know that a diner will tell him if something is wrong as soon as it becomes apparent, and not wait to be asked. Although yes, I am very much aware of the lingering resistance to abandoning the English nonsense of moaning among themselves about the toughness of the meat, the flaccidity of the veg, and then, when the waiter

A waiter of the sort one could probably do without: too assured,
too oily by half. And the drink? It is perhaps all the poor and put-upon
diner feels that at this stage of the meal he can honestly stretch to …

blithely canters up to seek assurance that everything in the garden is lovely, vying with one another to protest with enthusiasm the meal's magnificence. This simply must stop – because if something is wrong, the waiter must be told: he is not clairvoyant, nor even necessarily intuitive, and therefore deserves the opportunity to rectify the matter. One more thing that service should not be is in any way inept. If you are in the sort of restaurant that goes in for the delightfully showy business of the synchronized whisking-away of silver domes – well then synchronized it truly must be: no good one dozy fellow getting around to it seconds after the others, in the manner of Corporal Jones coming to attention. And we do not require the dropping of plates (particularly full ones, and even more particularly into laps), and neither sloppy pouring.

Nor must a waiter be remiss: if the restaurant is one of those that believes you are not to be trusted with your own bottles of wine and water, then these must appear regularly so that glasses are never empty (although you can always opt out of this largely unwelcome element of theatre by simply requesting that the bottles remain within your own reach). And the destination of each plate should be made plain and got straight by the waiter at the time of ordering so that no one is presented with someone else's meal – and nor do we want the flow further interrupted by his calling out, 'Who's the halibut …?' Moreover, while it is nice if the waiter remembers your name, it is quite unforgiveable for him to call you by that of someone else entirely. And although one does not want to be hurriedly bullied through each successive course at a breakneck pace, nor does one relish idling away aeons between the starter and the main … though to be fair, this is not the waiter's responsibility: he will serve a dish as soon as the kitchen presents it at the pass, so timing is really up to the sous-chef and the maître d'.

The bill must be delivered when it is asked for … and then the follow-up with the card machine should not be long in coming. Similarly, if a pudding menu or the return of the drinks list is requested, the implicit idea is that pudding and drinks will soon be ordered – so it's nice if the waiter thinks to return in order to ascertain one's requirements. And if you are not quite ready to order and request just two more minutes, it is desirable for the waiter to return just two minutes later, and not give way to either sulking or amnesia so that by the time of his eventual return you have visibly aged. There is another thing we don't want waiters to do – but it's not their fault when they very tiresomely go through it all, for they have been drilled and trained by management: 'Hey, you guys! My name is Jason, and I shall be looking after your table for the evening!' This is made rather worse should Jason hunker down as he says it, so that your face now becomes on the level of his flashing teeth and artificial enthusiasm (or – more scary – genuine enthusiasm). And Jason really must not be surprised nor aggrieved when no one responds by cheerily calling out, 'Hi, Jason! Really pleased to hear that!' because he just has to understand that it's not as if anyone actually gives the slightest damn in hell as to what his bloody name is. And if a waiter is to tell you the day's specials, it is better if the list is short enough to assimilate, and delivered in intelligible English. Further: when the food is delivered, he must not say, 'Enjoy!' (though he probably will).

So there is all that service should not be. And what it should be, in a word, is invisible. Dishes come and go, bread, water and wine are miraculously replenished, the table is decrumbed, fresh napkins descend as from heaven, and the conversation at the table is never for a moment broken: all this happens seamlessly, apparently lacking the agency of any human hand, and within a welcome cocoon of silence. Here, then, is true service ... and so by way of contradiction to my earlier statement: you *don't* actually know it when you see it, do you? Because really, you shouldn't be seeing it at all.

See also: BILL, COMPLAINING, ETIQUETTE, FRONT OF HOUSE, MENUS, ORDERING, PASS, PRESENTATION, REGULAR HAUNTS, SOMMELIERS, WINE LIST

SHARING

While the older generation is really very covetous of its plate of food – the escargots or oysters may be volubly praised, but no offer of one of the slippery little devils will ever be forthcoming – younger diners just lately are terribly into the whole egalitarian idea of sharing, maybe largely because it often favours fingers over cutlery. Sharing may be either the very concept and basis of a meal – tapas, *cichetti*, dim sum – or more loosely arranged around the understanding of everyone feeling free to pitch in: swooping down upon any plate but your own as a Brighton seagull to a sodden bag of vinegary chips in the mitt of someone who is about to be frightened witless. Which is all fine and dandy, so long as everyone has been adequately forewarned and is utterly agreeable – for there is nothing more maddening than being asked for a taster of whatever it is you are hoggishly enjoying, because it is virtually impossible to say no, and then inevitably they will alight upon the very little favourite titbit that you were consciously saving till last. Lovers will habitually sample each other's food (fingers again), and specialize in not just deliberately encouraging goo to trickle down their chins, but also spooning it with lascivious care into an open and willing mouth, yum yum yum. And restaurant critics will often commandeer a morsel of this or that from the plate of their 'companion', and particularly so if thus far the meal has proved to be barren of any interest or diversion whatsoever, and the desperation for copy of any sort is becoming insistent. Try not to be the person (woman) who says, 'No, I shan't order any chips, but I'll just have one of yours.' Because you'll have more than one, as well you know. And try not to be the person (man) who says, 'No, I shan't order a crème brûlée, but I'll just have one spoonful of yours.' Because you'll have more than one, as well you know.

See also: CHINESE, CHIPS, ETIQUETTE, EXCUSE FINGERS, LITTLE PLATES, ORDERING, PUDDING, ROMANCE, YOUNG PLACES

Already it is difficult to remember the days when a restaurant would offer the choice of 'smoking' or 'non-smoking' – let alone the golden era of personal freedom when anyone could puff away to their heart's content where and when they damn well pleased. Initially, it was not intended to extend the ban to private members' clubs, although this planned exemption was very soon jettisoned by those politicians who came to see such a measure as an open invitation to accusations of elitism. And so, members who collectively owned and hitherto had run their clubs according to the wishes of its subscribing members were forbidden to smoke anywhere within their own premises (this, of course, to include the fabled 'smoking rooms') – though for a time there remained just two exceptions to this draconian ruling. Any guesses …? Yes indeed: the House of Commons and the House of Lords, the very enactors of the law.

Most of the better and richer clubs have since invested fortunes in creating conducive partially covered, heated and comfortably furnished terraces … but for the working men's clubs, few of which could have afforded such a venture, the death knell sadly was tolling: the cheapness of supermarket beer and the freedom to smoke in one another's houses led a lot of lifelong members to abandon the clubs they had loved, this leading many of them into terminal decline, if not outright bankruptcy. Pubs responded to the new edict with the beer garden … or the car park … or the doorstep … or the scuzzy bit outside the loos around the back where they kept the bins and empty aluminium barrels – each of these dodgy venues choked with smokers and kiddies (who now, of course, were forced into passively gulping down far more carcinogenic tar than formerly). Before pubs and bars came to cater to the comfort of their more openly addicted patrons, it became common to sight a windswept huddle of smokers, spattered by the rain and blue with the cold, sucking down the nicotine while consoling themselves with the much-repeated mantra that all the best, most interesting, funniest and sexiest people were smokers, and hence in the great outdoors and at the mercy of the elements was the only place to be! Yes … and if cancer didn't get them, then pneumonia was never far away.

In proper restaurants, the law was largely greeted with approval and relief – for we all agree that it was never at all pleasant to be tackling the hors d'oeuvre just as four red and bibulous blokes at the next table were firing up the post-prandial Havanas. But wherever you find yourself now, a certain etiquette is to be observed by smoker and putative passive smoker alike. If there is no outside space, the decision is made for you: no smoking. But should you find yourself on a pleasant terrace or in a garden on a warm afternoon or evening, although smoking will be perfectly legal and sanctioned by the establishment, it is not just polite but actually essential to ask whether anyone in the immediate vicinity would terribly mind if you did. The light of fervent hope and desperate need will be alive in the smoker's eye as he near-pleadingly makes his heartfelt request … and it remains polite to smilingly give the go-ahead. If, however, you genuinely do violently object, then you should say so … though should you find yourself a minority of one amid a group of smokers, then you might consider retiring indoors – accommodatingly and with a disarming smile, however: not in a huff.

There is, of course, room for legal compromise: many restaurants and clubs have ample room to cater to smokers indoors without non-smokers being even aware of their presence in the building. But will any government of the future actually repeal the law? Something of a pipe dream, I feel.

See also: **CLUBS, ETIQUETTE, GASTROPUBS, OUTDOOR EATING**

SOFT OPENINGS

A soft opening is a bit like a theatre preview: it's all very nearly there, but the producer and director just have to be sure. They will listen to the views of selected playgoers, judge the levels of laughter and applause, and then maybe tweak the production accordingly.

Restaurant soft openings are usually held between one and three weeks prior to the official first day, often more as a final live-training exercise for the staff than anything else – although the more sympathetic restaurant critics will be informally invited (though there is a tacit understanding that no review will appear until they have dined there when the place is properly and officially up and running) and so too will regular patrons of any of the owner's existing restaurants, along with a motley of the usual foodie suspects. The meals are generally offered at half the normal price – although, as ever, certain highly prized people will receive no bill whatsoever: wouldn't you just know it? Unto he who hath a brief to eat out every single day of his bleeding life, shall be given buckshee grub.

SOLO DINING

'I hate to eat alone'. You seldom hear anyone saying that, nowadays – and I'm not at all convinced that the people who used unceasingly to tell you this ever were actually averse to the reality of solo dining per se, so much as being *seen* to be eating alone, and therefore tacitly classified by a knowing restaurant chock-full of convivial parties chowing down together (not to say lovey-dovey spooning couples feeding each other) as a true and unsavoury pariah, a veritable Norman No-Mates who very probably could bore for England and is likely possessed of exceedingly poor standards in personal hygiene, not to say highly suspect if not actually criminal sexual peccadilloes. But now – we are just all so cool with it. We swing by, rock up to the bar and order a glass of bubbly, half-a-dozen native oysters ... sprawl at a table on the pavement with a selection of little plates ... because we are leading a full and busy metropolitan life, see, and this quick little bite to eat is no more than just one more expression of it: fitted in – on the hoof, on the spur of the moment ... and on our own. Of course the iPad or hand-held 'device' is a great help: you can always appear to be involved, even when you are not remotely – seemingly crucially in touch with the whole of the world (yes, but please do note that it is when you are alone and *only* when you are alone that any such gadget may appear on the table: in company, these remain a no-no). The essential prop used to be the paperback in the old days – although pretending to read a novel more or less testified to the depth of your solitary indolence. But on a screen you can pretend to be *writing* a novel (or chairing an international meeting … or starting an international war).

It still is true, though, that the traditional restaurant is not all that keen on the solo diner – not any more to the extent that they would hustle the errant leper on to the deadliest table in the murkiest corner (and particularly if female, and therefore a prostitute), but purely on economic grounds: you are taking a table that could accommodate at least one further diner, and are unlikely to go through the full three courses, nor linger over a whole bottle of wine. On the plus side from their point of view, you will be in and out fast, and then with a bit of luck they can resell the table to proper people. But the practice of eating alone is not to be discounted: on occasion, it can be very pleasurable. You don't have to struggle to be witty and entertaining, you don't have to appear interested in uninteresting things, you can order precisely what you please without being in the slightest bit concerned about how it will 'look', and actually savour the wine and not just be necking it down … and all the while you are seemingly intent upon your screen, but actually eagerly listening in on everyone else's business, love affairs, secrets, lies and breakdowns, while simultaneously striving to subdue the reactive amazement in your giveaway eyeballs. *See also*: ETIQUETTE

SOMMELIERS

There is just one simple fact that you must never forget: it is the job of the sommelier to sell you wine. Yes, his expertise is to be consulted; yes, he should know better than to present you with a taster unless he previously has satisfied himself by way of a cork-sniff or taster of his own that the bottle is sound … but the restaurant does not employ so august a body as a fully-fledged sommelier (as distinguished by the discreet little bunch of grapes in the buttonhole of often a tailcoat) simply to applaud your choice, decant and pour correctly: it is the job of the sommelier to sell you wine. Most often, it is he who will have been in charge of buying it, and daily he has to justify those choices: and that means selling it. Which is achieved in a variety of ways. Initially there is the delicious clinking of the approaching champagne cart: a fabulous tureen bristling with tantalizing and perfectly chilled bubbly – the ideal aperitif, yes? Well yes, actually. But before you order, you're hardly going to ask the price of a flute, are you? No, you're not – and he knows this, you see. So already he has sold you some wine. And do know that a couple of glasses can easily be thirty quid or more: Lordy, you haven't even started the meal, and already you have no idea what is going on.

And if there is a proper sommelier, there surely will be a proper wine list: were you to study this to the extent that its breadth and quality doubtless deserve, you would grow old in your chair and simply die. So what to do? Well, the general procedure is to pick a colour and a nationality. Then you scroll through the regions while keeping a weather eye on the right-hand column of prices. Wince if you must, but do try not to gasp. If you are in a top-class restaurant for the bargain lunch, the wine will be pricey: that is part of how the restaurant makes up its margins … and it is the job of the sommelier to sell you wine. So if you jab at your choice with firmness of purpose and then decisively slam shut the weighty and considerable volume, that will be the end of the matter (unless you are later conveyed the doleful news that regrettably they have sold the last bottle – often the way, actually, and particularly at the cheaper end). Should you visibly waver, however, then instantly the sommelier will pounce upon your indecision and inform you that while the wine over which your finger still is trembling is perfectly all right in its way, rather forward in its class, a thoroughly reasonable example of the year … he nonetheless feels bound to point out that he is utterly convinced that you will find this alternative just here a great deal more rewarding. And will this alternative be more expensive? Well, let me see now: what do you think? It is the job of the sommelier to sell you wine.

The thing is not to be in any way intimidated or browbeaten, but still by all means make full use of his undoubted vast knowledge, if truly you wish to explore the list – and if that list is the main attraction of the place, then surely you will need no encouragement. If you request his advice outright, he should express an interest in what you have ordered to eat … and if he refers to the wines by their numbers, he's not much good. Later, he will dangle the empty bottle between fingers – or else glance over sadly at the spent decanter – and raise an enquiring eyebrow: up to you, how you react. Later yet, he will suggest a glass of maybe Sauternes to accompany your Stilton or pudding. And the wagon of liqueurs can hardly be far behind. Do not begrudge him this role: here is his theatre, the stage for his expertise, his *raison d'être*. Enter into the spirit of the thing and embrace it wholly … while never forgetting that it is the sommelier's job to sell you wine.

See also: APERITIF, BARGAIN LUNCH, BILL, COMPLAINING, DRINKING, LIQUID LUNCH, SERVICE, WINE LIST

SPANISH

Depending upon your outlook, it is the Spanish who are to be either praised or blamed for the proliferation of 'little plates' simply everywhere you look. Tapas rules! And not just in Spanish restaurants. But the conviviality of a tapas bar is hard to beat, so no wonder this simple concept has proved to be so contagious – and particularly when there is a gang of people looking for somewhere fun, informal and impromptu. The best waiters in these places seem always to be as enthusiastic as you are hungry, nodding with keenness at each of your choices, quickly asking whether you would like this or another dish as well, virtually applauding when you say you do – and then asking eagerly if maybe you want this one also ... and this one, and this one, and maybe too a glass of fino (blimey, though: you don't expect the Spanish Inquisition). Tapas meals are never as cheap as you think they are going to be – but always as cheerful, and still good value. Some places will advertise a flamenco evening. I leave it up to you to decide whether you wish to eat your meal amid the swirl and strumming of a flamenco evening: in my opinion, at dinner time a little castanet and Cuban-heeled stomping can go quite a long way. And, very quietly, the Spanish have been making very severe inroads into the world of fine dining. There is not yet too much evidence of this in Britain, but restaurants in Spain are regularly featuring prominently in, if not topping, lists of the finest places to eat in the world ... and honestly, I don't mean to be deflationary when I caution you to view all such lists with a degree of circumspection: the hoo-ha – not to say the cost – will often leave you wondering.

See also: FINE DINING, LITTLE PLATES, SERVICE, VALUE, WORLD'S 50 BEST RESTAURANTS

SPECIAL REQUIREMENTS

This really rather spooky phrase is creeping in everywhere. If ever you are invited to a formal dinner, awards ceremony or even a casual birthday get-together, the organizers feel bound by not just conscience but also the threat of subsequent litigation to cover their backs – and hence the request somewhere at the foot of the invitation: 'Please let us know if you have any special requirements'. To which the jokey answer is, Yes! Too much good grub and booze, please, ho ho ho! But what it normally comes down to is: are you a vegetarian or vegan? But it also can mean: are you intolerant? Not of your ex-partner, the cult of celebrity, useless politicians, the misuse of the apostrophe and bloody life in general – no no no – but things like wheat, gluten and dairy products. And if you do suffer such a misfortune, maybe you ought to consider staying at home …? I mean, I don't intend to tell you what to do, here – but otherwise, doesn't it all become a little bit of a business, really? Because throughout the evening, despite all the assurances that you will have been given, still you'll be anxious that somewhere amid the feast there might be lurking a malevolent peanut. So why take the risk? Best on the whole to eat only at restaurants that are tried and tested.

See also: ORDERING, UNUSUAL, VEGETARIAN AND VEGAN

SQUEEZED MIDDLE

This does not refer to your hitherto ample girth as a result of a recent bout of belt-tightening (for whatever reason), but the periodic plight of those restaurants that may most handily be described as 'local': the ones that you have been going to for ages and are perfectly serviceable and possibly just around the corner – though you would not think of making a journey elsewhere for anything broadly similar. One of these might even be your regular haunt … but when times are bad, this is just the sort of place that is going to suffer most. Times of financial restraint never remotely affect the extremes of eating out: the famous and expensive star-chef restaurants will pretty much always be booked solid, while profits at the likes of McDonald's will effortlessly leap (they're lovin' it! And so, presumably, are the deluded punters). But if times are hard, the middle classes will tend to revert to home cooking (or ready meals, courtesy of the supermarkets' eternal 'dine-in' deals) and takeaways: suddenly, a tenner for a bowl of pasta (plus service) appears an extravagance.

Some restaurants in the squeezed middle jettison the lunchtime operation – because often the cost of simply opening the door, turning on the lights, firing up the kitchen and employing a single waitress will far outstrip the midday turnover, let alone margin – while others will decide that staying open every single hour that the good Lord grants them just has to be the answer. Many though, sadly, will go to the wall. And here is nothing so simple as the jungle rule of the survival of the fittest, for an extraordinary number of the truly direst places seem inexplicably to survive forever: most often it's the humble and blameless little trattoria that goes under – whereupon there will be, among local residents, much lamenting and rending of garments … However, although not directly their fault, such closures will be a result of sudden and necessary economies, and the falling away of their patronage. Sad, but true.

See also: REGULAR HAUNTS, STAR CHEFS, TAKEAWAYS

STAR CHEFS

A cook, if sufficiently hard-working and talented, can become a chef. A chef – if all of the above, as well as possessed of some or other instantly identifiable characteristic (not necessarily, or even desirably, attractive) and a healthy dose of luck, while simultaneously mainlining on the twin highs of television and publishing contracts – can then become a *star* chef … and from there it can be but a short hop, skip and a jump away from his becoming no more than just a star. For within the cocoon of his new-found and stellar fame, that chef by definition will no longer be cooking. Here is the eternal truth and conundrum central to every instance of over-promotion: the high-flyer pretty much entirely ceases to do the one and only thing in which he is supremely qualified, and that which was solely responsible for his dizzying rise in the first place. I can think of a few new chefs on the London restaurant scene who might yet prove to be welcome exceptions to this pretty grim scenario … but I dare not name them, for fear that by the time you are reading these words, all will be different (because a week may, as they say, be a long time in politics, but in restaurant-land it is very nearly an era).

There did exist a time, buried deep within our innocent past, when such as Gordon Ramsay and Marco Pierre White were young, industrious, fiercely ambitious and highly talented chefs toiling away night and day in their respective much-lauded kitchens. Then their names were spattered across a dozen restaurant facades, a stack of books and a slew of prime-time programmes, while even more lucratively fronting a malevolence of ads and endorsements. And these days … one wonders whether they remember even how to turn on the gas. There have been a few more since who have gone the same way; and here is a very good reason to get yourself down to a suddenly vaunted restaurant with a hot new talent in the kitchen before the PR boys, TV executives and literary agents rumble and bombard them with irresistible temptation. Because after that, matey – forget it: they'll be off.

But restaurants boasting star chefs – even if in name only – will always be a massive draw, though of course the very best of them still have the advertised chef actually cooking in the kitchen (if not all the time, then at least in the evenings). Michel Roux Jr and Raymond Blanc, despite their overwhelming television and publishing commitments, still seem to manage to get their hands dirty, and very apparently just love it. Michael Caines, Bryn Williams, Angela Hartnett, Marcus Wareing, Rowley Leigh, Tom Kitchin, Andrew Fairlie, Philip Howard, Brett Graham, Mark Hix … all these Michelin-starred chefs and more still like nothing more than the cut and thrust of the infernal kitchen (where they sure can stand the heat), and it is very worthwhile to seek them out. Booking will never be easy – and particularly for the bargain lunch – but if ever a boat has truly to be pushed out, it is in a star-chef establishment that it ought to be done. If only because following service, very often the star of the show, the main event, will don his signature whites and do a lap of honour of his restaurant, glad-handing the adorers, doling out autographs and maybe even posing for a picture: all this just knocks the punters dead, both chefs and diners visibly loving the theatre and thrill of it all. But the real point is, of course, that the cooking, service and presentation in such places is (or damn well ought to be) the very best there is.

See also: BARGAIN LUNCH, BOOKING, FINE DINING, MENUS, RESTAURANT GUIDES, SERVICE, VALUE

STEAK

In recent years, steak has stepped out from the shadows of dull predictability to become wholly rehabilitated as, believe it or not, something new and very cool. The slab of cow receives this entry all to itself – as very few disparate ingredients do – partly because for just ever steak and chips has been cited as the nation's favourite restaurant choice. Preceded by prawn cocktail, followed by a stodgy wodge of Black Forest gateau, accompanied by either a gallon of red or several of beer, and rounded off so very terribly nicely with a large, thick breakfast cup of filter. Probably only men would actually have specified all of this, and admittedly a fairly long time ago (the whole of the foregoing menu pretty much summing up the A–Z ethos of Berni Inn, from days of yore). But steak has progressed from being seen as the default selection by those of limited palate and who really don't get out enough.

No longer do we live in a world where the steak on offer just had to be either rump (good enough flavour, could be as chewy as hell) or sirloin (equally decent flavour, usually tenderish … but you got less actual meat for your money than if you went for rump, and also there was that collar of fat running the whole length of the thing that you were paying for by weight but would be a fool to yourself to actually contemplate eating), and then finally fillet (neat and lean, not tasting of too much, and so bleeding small you could actually go through three of them with ease). And that was half the trouble with 'slap-up' meals in those days: despite the additional padding of a few tiny and ice-cold prawns and much shredded lettuce engulfed in pink gloop, frozen 'fries', peas and mushrooms from tins and then a slab of gooey cake … there wasn't in total all that much food. As a consequence, families who ate out very little were frequently left dissatisfied as they kissed goodbye to near enough a week's wages, feeling not just peeved, but also actually rather peckish.

But now: steak is big, clever and fashionable. Steak is the choice of the cosmopolitan connoisseur who is willing to pay a massive chunk of dosh for a similarly proportioned hunk of beef – rare breed, aged and cooked uncommonly well. A lot of this is to do with the United States: visiting Americans were always putting down our steaks and burgers (quite rightly) and then began opening their own places, such as Christopher's in Covent Garden. Which, if ever you have madly strayed into an Angus Steak House (still with us, rather eerily), you will agree could only be a good thing. While all brasseries and most restaurants now offer more than one steak option, there are also the chains and specialists: not just American, but also Argentinian, British and, a bit weirdly, Russian. Unusual Scottish breeds, as well as such as Wagyu and Kobe (the animals are massaged, fed like kings and generally live a far better life than you do), will be presented in their raw state for you to okay and issue precise instructions as to how they should be cooked. Which is always a difficult thing to convey precisely – because one man's rare is another man's blue. In America, it is more of an exact science: I remember a steak house in Chicago that offered twenty gradations of cooking, from literally raw as a tartare to virtually incinerated. If you specified number 11, say, but in your estimation the steak before you was a 12, they would whisk it away and start again: only in the US of A. And one more word about tartare: do only order this in a restaurant that you absolutely trust as to the freshness of ingredients, and with a chef or head waiter utterly competent in proper chopping, seasoning and judicious binding with raw egg – otherwise you will have on your hands something that is at the very least actively disgusting, if not potentially lethal.

Everyone cherishes a memory of their best steak ever: on no account dream of fashioning this into an anecdote, let alone a running narrative (and 'knowledgeable' is quite as bad as 'amusing'). Because there are steak bores just as there are burger bores and wine bores, and you really do not want to be one of those.

See also: BRASSERIE, BURGERS, CHAINS, CHIPS, VALUE

SUNDAY ROAST

I think that a considerable fortune, with commensurate publicity and gratitude, might await the restaurant that is willing to offer a Sunday roast 'with all the trimmings' ... on Wednesday: so often round about midweek that does strike me as a delightful idea, but (with the noble exception of Simpson's-in-the-Strand) it can be the very devil to find. While on Sundays, of course, it's rather hard to order anything else – for here is the day's special just everywhere, from the top hotels to the humblest gastropub by way of a surprising number of brasseries, who also seem to feel that they are duty-bound to cater to the trad-itional Sabbath appetite. One can understand the allure from both sides, really: if a restaurant lays on a vast joint of beef and maybe one of pork and lamb as well, each portion works out really very eco-nomically, the veg and Yorkshire not adding much at all to the overall cost of the dish. The diners, meanwhile, may lick their chops (as it were) at the prospect of the coming 'slap-up' feed while being liber-ated from all the palaver of actually creating the thing from scratch, and still manage to feel rather virtuous about sitting around a table with maybe all the family – just like they used to do in the old days. Except I really do feel that the Sunday roast is the one meal that still really ought to be freshly prepared at home, there to be enjoyed: but that's just me, I know. If you are moved to venture out for Sunday lunch, however, do make it somewhere good – or, better still, make it somewhere splendid. The grand hotels remain the best bet, especially if they are doing a prime rib of beef (on the bone, obviously), because unless your family is Mormon in proportion, that's a great rarity at home. Sunday roasts in pubs are ostensibly tempting and undeniably good value, but can have something of the school dinner about them ... the merest whiff of the sanatorium.

See also: FAMILY MEALS, GASTROPUBS, HOTELS, VALUE

TABLES

The British have views about tables in restaurants … well – only one view, actually, and it goes like this: put me in a corner. Or, failing that, against the wall. Don't even for a minute imagine that you're going to stick me in the middle of this enormous room where people are going to be *looking* and constantly walking past me on all four sides, because then I'm going to be exceedingly jumpy. And particularly so if I happen to be a woman because my handbag is going to be on the floor beside me but I shan't at all feel that it's *safe* … There are, of course, other deal-breaking provisos within the corner/wall stipulation: I do not want to be next to the door to the street because every time it opens I shall feel forced to look up and then quickly look away again as soon as my glance is met – and also there will be one bugger of a draught. And nor do I want to be next to the loos. Obviously. And I certainly don't want to be shoved upstairs where the rail of coats is, nor thrown down into the basement where something is ominously humming, when clearly the correct and fun place to be is on the ground floor proper. And I didn't either ever used to want to be anywhere in the vicinity of the kitchen, but now that so often we are confronted with a stainless-steel open feature and I am told that it is something of a privilege to be able to witness the sweaty chefs at their labours, I am now just a little confused and frankly undecided on the matter (though if I am being absolutely honest, I'd still rather not, if it's all the same to you).

If you are in your regular haunt, you will want not just a 'good' table – but *your* table: the one you make for without being told. And if you truly are a regular, then you are quite entitled to expect it … but do understand that if you haven't booked but just popped in on the off chance, it is unfair to demand it … and also know that – especially if we are talking about a fashionable place with a high-profile clientele – 'your' table will be someone else's also: unpalatable, but there it is. So sometimes the beleaguered front of house will have to indulge in a fair amount of judicial juggling, but of course will always do his very utmost on your behalf (or so, anyway, he will assure you). If you are in an unfamiliar restaurant and are conducted to a table that for any reason you dislike, do try to say so immediately: if the place is packed and none other is available, then you must make your choice – sit, or walk.

And now to the business of table settings. This used to be uncontentious, all tables being much of a muchness in terms of what they sported and the way in which they were all laid out: not so today. Some people could not give a hang about any of this, but to those who do it is of vital importance: they will not knowingly book a restaurant that flaunts a naked table, because cloths are seen to be essential. Also proper napkins – i.e. not paper. But if they must be paper, then let them be the large, thick, sheeny and faintly lineny variety and not the tiny translucent thing, through which any droppage twixt cup and lip will pass unhesitatingly, as if through a riddle. People to whom all of this is significant will also appreciate a nod in the direction of fresh flowers (and a candle in the evening), weighty cutlery and particularly gleaming stemware, the rims of which are as thin as thin. And butter that isn't wrapped. And, not at all incidentally, that the table itself is as far away from any other as is possible without its being in a different room altogether. And that the chairs around said table are not giving their lower back a fair bit of gyp, but encourage them to sprawl and linger. While the people who couldn't care a fig for all that (let us call them 'the young') not only put up with but also would actively prefer to be squatting on a hard wooden shelf or stool before a bare, shared and maybe sticky table – the single knife and fork placed on top of an idiot napkin folded into a triangle, or else slung into a miniature galvanized bucket. It will not bother them that the glasses are as thick as a window pane, and greyly dappled with the residue of solvent from a dishwasher that is a stranger to the final rinse programme. And should the food arrive on a lump of greasy wood or a slab of slate, this is so much to the good: one suspects that the arrival of a communal manger would be greeted with much stamping of the feet and whoops of open delight.

So: know your restaurant, and the way they lay things out.

See also: BOOKING, BREAD AND BUTTER, COMFORT, DECOR, FASHION, FRONT OF HOUSE, KITCHEN TABLE, LOOS, PRESENTATION, REGULAR HAUNTS, SERVICE, YOUNG PLACES

TAKEAWAY

Takeaway is the time-honoured compromise between eating out and staying in: you aren't in a restaurant, but a restaurant has cooked your food. The pluses are clear: it's considerably cheaper, you don't have to get dressed and faff around with transport … and if you are feeling really very slobby indeed, you can even dispense with dishes (and therefore the washing-up). On the downside, the actual food – though serviceable, because by now, via a process of elimination, you will have found a local Chinese, Indian or, at a pinch, Italian that suits you – well … it's never going to be show-stopping, is it? And particularly if rendered claggy on eventual arrival because the delivery person persists in getting lost and will keep on putting through increasingly hysterical phone calls to see where you are and you tell him repeatedly and tetchily that you are where you always have been but more to the point where in bloody hell is *he*?!

Then there are the secret takeaways: those that no one is meant to know about (with the exception, as ever, of those in the know). There are certain well-known brasseries and even Michelin-starred restaurants that will, for favoured customers, discreetly deliver a fabulous meal, beautifully presented and even served for you, if you wish. At a price, needless to say. And although of course they would never be so vulgar as to advertise such a service … it's always worth asking. Your casual request might be met with a blank look of genuine incomprehension, outright refusal – or else pleasantly surprising compliance.

See also: PIZZA

TEA

Tea is the new breakfast. For a long time now it has been seen to be rather cool to meet people somewhere rather glamorous for a breakfast piece of business, or maybe a romantic farewell following a rumpled night of torrid doings (neither of which should be attempted in a cafe or greasy spoon). Recently, however, tea has become more the thing, this new sort of ceremony being particularly favoured by women (ladies who tea …?) because it fits in so well with shopping, and they love the huge variety of specialist teas that these days are offered as a matter of course (bright emerald peppermint in a clear glass pot being always a favourite) … and they also love scones. With cream and jam. And – no matter what they say – they also love cake.

'Tea at the Ritz' is so famous a phrase as to seem almost the title of a classic novel – and as a result of its international renown, this beautiful room is booked up whole seasons in advance. But there are many other quite fabulous places to take tea, and London, for once, by no means holds the monopoly: here is where a country hotel worth anything at all can and should seize the opportunity and be truly outstanding. But in London, posh tea is very much the province of the grand hotels and fashionable brasseries – where a table at four o'clock can be quite as difficult to acquire as one for lunch or dinner. Do always go to a place where the perfectly precisely cut little sandwiches, freshly baked scones and pretty coloured cubes of cake are presented vertically upon a charming three-tiered display stand: it just ain't the same if it don't stack up. Do not always – or ever – resist the offer of a glass of champagne. And if you are offered a finger sandwich, do not say, 'Well actually, I'd on the whole be much more happy with ham, or maybe cucumber.'

See also: BOOKING, BRASSERIE, BREAKFAST, CAFES, GREASY SPOONS, HOTELS, LADIES WHO LUNCH, ROMANCE

By which I do not mean restaurants within theatres (which, rather oddly to my mind, are yet to be invented – it must simply be to do with the lack of space), but those usually time-honoured places that are clustered close to theatres in provincial towns and throughout London's theatre-land, nearly all of which wisely have adjusted their menu and hours in order to accommodate the playgoer. Because 'curtain up' has always played merry hell with the epicure's digestion, many having given up the unequal struggle with timing and plumping instead for a proper and leisurely dinner, and to hell with whatever happens to be on at Drury Lane. But there are quite a few venerable establishments – J. Sheekey springs to mind, and particularly so since the opening of their terrific adjoining oyster bar – where you can be served a starter and main at, say, six o'clock ... and then toddle back after the play for cheese or pudding, coffee and cognac (and – in the old days – a damned fine cigar): and they stay open later than most, these places.

If the restaurant is literally next door to a theatre, as many are, you could even nip back in during the interval for a swift glass of something one hell of a lot better and almost certainly cheaper than anything you're going to get in a crush bar (always assuming you actually manage to barge and pummel your way to the counter before the second-act bell is sounding shrilly in your ears). One solid reason why there has been a considerable falling off in the traditional fully-fledged big night out comprising dinner and theatre is that if you combine the cost of these while factoring in taxis, maybe trains, conceivably babysitters and then a few drinks beforehand and afterwards ... well then the resultant mega-figure tends to involve the instant remortgaging of one's home, and many have decided that, on balance, they would prefer a roof over their head to a segmented meal scythed through the centre by either the stomping hilarity of such as *Mamma Mia!*, or else the relentlessness of the latest lengthy polemic from the likes of David Hare.

THEFT

Huge and heartfelt gratitude is due from the aficionado of eating out (who is yourself, presumably) to the great Sir Terence Conran. He was the man who first brought to London all the swagger and bedazzle of the glittering Paris brasserie and the Austrian grand cafe in the form of the subterranean Quaglino's (more than twenty years ago now). And although he paved the way for so much glory to come, as most usually exercised by Jeremy King and Chris Corbin of Wolseley fame, and Richard Caring of J. Sheekey and the Ivy, along with many others … it is also to Sir Terence we must turn when apportioning blame for the ever burgeoning crime scene that restaurant-land very quickly became. For in Quaglino's (Quags to its chums) there was on every table what was instantly and collectively perceived to be quite simply the most nickable ashtray in the universe: a chunky little zinc job in the form of the trademark 'Q' – and, in anticipation of its allure, actually offered for sale on the menu, so optimistic a gesture at a stroke rendering the stealing of it an apparently irresistible challenge. And although he bemoaned his spiralling weekly losses (scores of the things were disappearing daily), I think that Terence must secretly have been highly amused, and incidentally wholly delighted by the endless reams of free publicity that all this wholesale larceny quite effortlessly engendered.

Certainly all of his many subsequent restaurants boasted a 'collectable' zinc ashtray, and many people made it a point of honour to visit every Conran restaurant, if only the once, solely with the highly dishonourable purpose of relieving it of an ashtray. And although ashtrays now in these pure and smokeless days are no more than a thing of fondest memory (along with all those legitimately takeable books of matches), the unscrupulous punter will always find something to nick – and the more fashionable and upmarket the establishment, the more vulnerable such items find themselves. Because nobody is going to swipe a Duralex glass or thick ceramic teacup from a greasy spoon, are they? But lay before the light-fingered diner monogrammed linen napkins, silver cruets, handsomely bound menus, dinky little tea strainers, escargot forklets, or any plate or saucer bearing the motif or brand of the place, and said sod knows no bounds. The justification is always the same with thieves: they've got hundreds of the things – they'll never miss just one ... they can afford it, Christ knows they charge enough in here ... they ought to thank me: it's free publicity! All pretty shoddy behaviour, I'm sure you'll agree: because let's face it – you are never going to stoop to such a thing, are you? Of course not: I knew that. No no – I'm not being sarcastic, truly I'm not. I mean it. Sincerely.

See also: **BRASSERIE, FASHION**

TIPPING

'A discretionary service charge of 12½% will be added to your bill'. So ubiquitous and utterly commonplace this phrase has become as to be hardly even worthy of attention. But it's all in that key word 'discretionary': here is not an obligatory extra levy (and 12½ per cent of restaurant prices is these days always considerable) but an optional gratuity, notionally for service. If the service you received was disgraceful – and should that be the case, you don't so much want to leave a tip as clunk the rude and useless sod around the side of the head with the carafe he so very cack-handedly managed to pour over the crotch of your trousers – then one hopes that you will not be forced to strike off the charge ... because the restaurant would be aware, and beat you to it. Maybe. But never remove the charge if service was adequate, because it's simply rather mean.

What quite rightly exercises people are these two things (or at least they should do, anyway). First, the iniquity of every establishment applying the service charge to a bill that already contains 20 per cent VAT: do you really want to tip HM Revenue & Customs for having taxed you? You do not – but there seems to be no way around it. The other factor is whether the money does actually go to the waiting staff, or simply becomes just more bunce for the restaurant. The answer is that it all depends: some restaurants will give the entire amount to the waiter or waitress, no question – though often this is to supplement shamefully low wages. Sometimes just an unspecified and occasionally fluctuating percentage of that percentage will find its way to the server, and sometimes all that day's gratuities are pooled into the so-called tronc to be shared out equally. In theory. The truth is, you never really can be sure. If you are particularly taken with a waiter's good service, however, ask him if he would prefer the tip in cash. If he expresses indifference, then the restaurant is operating a fair and generous policy. Should he positively leap at the idea, visibly slavering, then it rather would look as if the restaurant is pulling a fast one. But it's always worth having a bit of cash about your person so that you are at least in the position to extend the offer. And you may even feel moved to leave a fiver on the table as an extra, over and above the all-in charge: absolutely no obligation, of course – but if you intend using the restaurant again, or find yourself in a regular haunt, your kindness will be noted and remembered … very possibly to be repaid by way of other sorts of kindness in the future. And look on the bright side: in America, if ever you dream of tipping less than 20 per cent, you may fully expect to be the recipient of a steak knife stuck firmly between your mean little shoulders.

See also: BILL, REGULAR HAUNTS, SERVICE

TRAVEL EATING

Eating while on the move has very evidently improved immeasurably … and then again, it hasn't. In that some of us remember when air travel was possessed of style, glamour, even a certain swagger – these now having been supplanted by fear, degradation, brain-warping humiliation and the frittering of so very much sweet and precious time

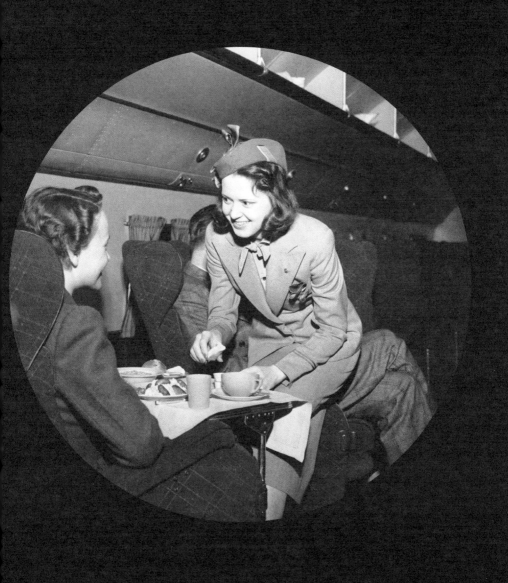

All the joys of early (1938) in-flight catering, not to mention a
wonderful example of female multitasking, with our eager-to-please
stewardess happily chatting away to the lady while also, equally happily,
apparently sitting on the lap of her chap. It's the only way to travel.

within a vacuum-packed dumpster. Unless, of course, you are rich. In which case, such nonsenses as queuing and being ritually frisked and glared at accusingly are blissfully unknown – and so too is a cling film-swaddled bap. In first-class airport lounges, everything short of Scarlett Johansson, George Clooney and a knighthood is at your disposal. The wise, well-heeled and seasoned traveller will arrive deliberately early – not enforcedly and under pain of punishment, like the rest of us – in order to avail himself of the myriad delights on offer in a cool, spacious and beautifully designed interior: really good vintage champagne and clarets, caviar, lobster, grills … as well as invigorating power showers, a valet … and even a masseuse (it's really just as well that the cattle classes know very little of all this, or else there might be triggered a bloody revolution – which is just about all your average airport is lacking). Foodie class distinctions continue on board, of course – the irony being that while those in steerage grapple with whatever is thrown with contempt in their general direction (some or other more or less unidentifiable thing, with a packet of infants' cutlery made from seemingly very similar ingredients), frequent flyers in First will frequently wave away the Dom Pérignon, the filet mignon, the Dover sole … They have no need of such petty perks, is the potent message – and anyway, as soon as the plane touches down their driver is whisking them to dinner at that legendary and fabulous restaurant where only they can be sure of a table. Cafes, general eateries and takeaways in airports can be pretty good (though not the ones that obviously are pretty bad), and you might think it best to eat at one of these before your flight, so as to be spared being victim to 'in-flight catering' – or else eat something on board that you yourself have prepared at home: not for the sake of economy, but in order just to know that at least you will be sure of having something decent.

Train travel is a rather different kettle of fish (cod, if you're very lucky indeed). In this country, we lament the passing of proper silver service. The Brighton Belle, say – upon which breakfast would be beautifully served to you by liveried waiters, despite the fact that there was never quite enough time actually to eat it, and on the final approach into Brighton there were violent bends that always ensured the slopping of the tea and coffee all over the fine white-linen napery. Lunches and dinners too on the old trains were very professionally and attractively served, but the food was fairly close to institutional: claggy soup, overdone everything else. Such luxury trains as the British Pullman and the Orient-Express are something else again: here you will receive a pretty wonderful meal (and if you look at the minuscule proportions of the galley kitchen, its production appears to be nothing short of miraculous) – though of course, this does come at a price. At railway stations these days you no longer are stuck with the tea urn and a slice of processed cheese slapped between two slabs of Sunblest: the takeaway scene now is generally reasonably good. Buying food on a train depends upon how desperately hungry you are (because you would have to be) and whether you can be bothered to stagger and be bounced like a pinball the length of four or five carriages in order to queue for a very expensive bacon roll that, due to its microwave-zapping, will scald your tongue and palate, and a plastic thing of coffee that, while not tasting remotely of coffee, will, however, scald your tongue and palate. Or there is the trundling trolley, which is stocked by people who remain convinced that as a nation we are fixated upon miniatures of spirits, muffins and packets of cheesy biscuits. On a point of etiquette, it is always preferable on concourse or train to eat in a designated area, and preferably at a table: the combination of other people's laptops, other people's iPods, other people's 'personal' phone calls and – the clincher – other people's crisps has been known to drive yet other people entirely to the very brink of murder.

Motorway service stations …? Avoid. Obviously. And then there is the cruise ship: the business of food on a cruise ship is utterly unparalleled anywhere else in the universe. While very few indeed might actually eat to cruise, the large (often very large indeed) majority will decidedly cruise to eat – the reason being, of course, that it is 'all-in' (an overriding reason why the cruise was booked in the first place).

Drink may not be included in the price, but grub most assuredly is. And so often what passes for etiquette and discretion while cruising is to be scoffing something down every single hour of the day and night without necessarily being seen to. So you will stagger your time of breakfast, say, so as not to keep colliding with the same old faces, each of which will at the time be stuffed with bacon. This breakfast being subsequent, of course, to early morning tea, toast and muesli. And not really that much prior to elevenses – leaving you more or less enough time for a well-earned sit-down on deck with a nice bag of sweeties before attending to the serious business of lunch. Then tea. Which will segue into pre-prandial nibbles – before the coming of the big one, El Gordo: dinner itself. The five or so courses leaving hardly any room to graze on savoury titbits and chocolates in the bar afterwards – where you must be careful not to doze off over your brandies, or else you might miss out on the nightly 'midnight feast' (force yourself – it would be antisocial not to). The conclusion of which would leave nothing whatsoever to look forward to until early morning tea, toast and muesli prior to a proper English breakfast ... so let us thank God, then, for cabin service, which dutifully operates throughout the night (and is very much called upon, you may depend on it).

See also: CAFES, ETIQUETTE, SERVICE, VALUE

TWISTS

Twists are much vaunted by chefs, who, quite frankly, can sometimes seem not to know exactly what they are meant to be doing. 'Traditional British – with a twist!' ... 'Pan-Asian – but with a little twist!' ... 'Classic provençale – but given a novel twist!' Why? Is the time-honoured original really not good enough? Twists do smack of desperation. For God's sake be told: leave all the twisting to Chubby Checker – stick to the straight and narrow.

See also: FUSION, MENUS

The word 'unusual' is used descriptively by the British rather in the way that they might loftily pronounce some or other thing to be 'interesting'. It means either that they are highly dubious, not so much interested as bored, or else that they haven't really been listening to much that's been going on. 'Unusual' is, by definition, unfamiliar – and therefore carries the undertone of threat: we won't immediately rush to rule it out altogether, but certainly we are going to sniff with suspicion and pad around the thing for a good long while before we even will think to embrace it. Because honestly: what would be your initial thought if someone said to you, 'By the way, there's this new restaurant you just have to go to: it is really unusual.' What you might say is, 'Unusual in what way?' but what you'd be thinking is, Well no, I don't really think so. As to decor, it's difficult now to think of anything that might any more be termed unusual, because we've had the bloody lot, quite frankly. Restaurants in not sufficiently converted lavatories, furnished from a skip; concrete bunkers; rusting metal; scaffolding; exposed plumbing; newspaper on the tables; flashing lights; no lights at all so that you have to be physically escorted to your eerie, funereal and frankly very worrying table; restaurants built of ice where you are lent a fur coat at the entrance; subterranean restaurants tricked out to resemble an Amazonian jungle; perfectly white and unadorned restaurants where the only decoration is the no-doubt highly decorative you … And so on. And so forth. We haven't yet had a restaurant with a Nazi-memorabilia theme, and nor one where you are required to strip naked at the door and carry a balloon in one hand and a daffodil in the other (I don't think), but every other sort of 'unusual' seems to have been pressed into service with varyingly escalating degrees of hysteria and desperation.

And so 'unusual' had then to percolate down to the menus themselves … and here is food that is more or less a dare. A challenge. A talking point, sure – but also a point of honour. At the very top end, we had the much-lionized Ferran Adrià, of elBulli fame, the Spanish restaurant that, before he closed it down, was constantly touted as the best in the world (by such people who feel compelled to rank restaurants in lists intended to reflect to the desperately insecure and impressionable their relative global magnificence), with a two-year waiting list for tables. It was he who first devised menus in a 'laboratory', resulting in such as wild flowers encased in translucent and edible paper, fine hams transformed into liquid, and – with the help of liquid nitrogen – certain foods made to look like other foods altogether: an endless succession of beautiful titbits, and an amazing spectacle, to be sure. Is it art? Oh, most definitely. But, more to the point: is it dinner? Anyway, all great fun, if cursedly expensive, but rather regarded by the sane as something that ought maybe to be experienced once, like Disneyland, say, or voting for the Lib Dems: certainly you can't rationally plan upon ever doing such a thing again.

Then there is all the rest of the gimmickry, rather further down the scale, which is consciously and wholly aimed at the only section of society that may be guaranteed to fall for all of this sort of baloney hook, line and sinker ... and we call this section of society 'men'. Because in this context, women are relatively balanced. And will not be queuing up to eat a chilli so hot that it is quite literally potentially lethal, and requires a signed disclaimer. Nor the legendary Japanese fugu fish, which can poison you in an instant, but needn't necessarily. Nor will they rush to eat locusts and scorpions no matter how crunchily fried, nor even ants – and who cares how richly 'enrobed' in chocolate they may be ...? So should you be confronted with a restaurant that has gone out of its way to look even more ludicrously hideous than the general run of the thing, that with its stoat and parsnip specials is striving to go far beyond mere 'fusion', that offers infinitely more bizarre avenues than might ever be approached by the inclusion of simple 'twists' ... you really must ask yourself: why? And – more to the point – whether actually you want to be there.

See also: COMFORT, DECOR, FUSION, INDIAN, MENUS, STAR CHEFS, TWISTS

In three words: you simply mustn't. Here is an evening not for eating out, but for cooking – whichever one of you is best at it. A romantic setting by all means: it is always far too cold for outside eating, so here is an opportunity to create your very own little piece of paradise within (though do not do what they do in the films and drape your lamps with chiffon scarves because they will smoulder and then catch light, and there is nothing so guaranteed to break the romantic mood as the front door being axed down by a bunch of firemen). The trouble is, however, women have now been indoctrinated into expecting to be taken out to dinner; men know this, and so with a lowering heart will attempt to book somewhere, if not to generate passion, then at least to keep the peace. And if they leave it too late, they're in trouble: the good places will be full – because on Valentine's Day, very depressingly, we have one of the busiest and most lucrative evenings in the restaurant calendar.

The usual menu will have been supplemented by a candle, a pink-ribboned napkin and very possibly an overpriced and underpowered cocktail called something along the lines of Love Potion No. 9, while prices generally are discreetly hoicked. And do have sympathy for anyone who was genuinely unaware of the pregnant importance of the night and has simply strayed in with a mate for a bite to eat … for they will be highly conspicuous amid a sea of dickied-up couples trying really bloody hard. It will rarely go well: self-consciousness will often get the better of a woman, while bill-consciousness can entirely immobilize her partner. There will be whoops from a corner as some happy female, following much fevered urging, successfully and stickily extricates an engagement ring from amid the depths of her crème brûlée; there will be scowls of resentment, the replaying of ancient arguments and possibly outright violence from another table where all such shenanigans have signally failed to take place. And people are watching: so why do you want to be on show? You don't want to be on show, do you? So someone's home is best, with a decent takeaway if you're not up to all the faff of the kitchen. And should the evening go well – and in such circumstances it stands a very good chance – well then it's all so very much more convenient, because you don't even have to dress.

See also: **CELEBRATIONS, ROMANCE**

VALUE

Our shoulders are stout enough to bear the disappointment of a meal that has failed to come up to scratch … we might eventually find it within our hearts to forgive the serial ineptitude of a hapless waiter … but the one thing we simply are not prepared to tolerate – the barb that will rankle within for quite possibly years – is a restaurant having ripped us off: that awful collapse of the stomach, the stale, sour taste in the mouth when you know deep inside that you have been well and truly kippered. People are far more likely to tell of bad experiences than good (unless the good was just truly sensational), but although tales of poor food and slipshod service might be recounted with a sense of wonder, or even humour, only anger and a great sense of grievance will do when convinced that we have been cheated and taken for fools. Because here is the point: we want the bill to be 'reasonable' not just for the sake of economy, but also because we require the satisfaction of a contract whose terms have been met by both parties – we just will not be seen to be idiots paying for sod all in return.

Value, however, by no means need mean cheap: some of the finest restaurants are obviously and famously expensive, but often (and particularly for the bargain lunch) offer very good value indeed. The costs involved in achieving a perfect plate of food impeccably served are simply colossal, and all that talent, attention to detail and sheer hard work can add up to an attractively good deal. Often it is in the cheaper places – the squeezed middle – where value can seem very poor: a pizza, a side, a glass of wine, a coffee … we don't really feel that we've had anything in the way of a spread, and the subsequent bill can often seem to be disproportionate. Because in cases such as this it's more about overheads, and far less about what is actually on your plate. Value, though, is a highly personal thing: if you are into wine and spot a very fine and rare bottle on the list, you might think that the high price on it actually represents excellent value; others would not so much as even consider it, believing the price to be extortionate. And you know when you've had good value, don't you? You glow with satisfaction: it is a good feeling … and one that is amply aided by the food and drink, of course.

See also: **BARGAIN LUNCH, BILL, OVERHEADS, SQUEEZED MIDDLE, WINE LIST**

VEGETABLES

Yes we like our meat – but please let us never forget the two veg. Or even more. Although these days, this could prove to be rather expensive: virtually everything now is classified as an optional 'side', and highly charged for accordingly – such calculating husbandry frequently extending even to the vital chips to accompany your steak (though they still do seem to come as a matter of course with any sort of battered or breadcrumbed fish). Three sides could easily cost as much as, if not more than, the main meal on your plate; the healthy option of five a day could pretty much wipe you out. Many fine-dining establishments will proudly create an entire and self-sufficient 'plat', and they can become really quite annoyed should you hanker after more veg on the top of it. French, I'm talking about, obviously – who never really have looked at vegetables the way the British do (i.e. as a proper plate-filling ingredient, and particularly so in the case of spuds, rather than simply as 'colour' or garnish). The French are beginning to wake up, though – the acclaimed chef Bruno Loubet having recently opened a restaurant in London where the vegetables are the star of the show, with meat and fish reduced to merely spear-carrying bit players.

In a bistro or brasserie you'll be fine with the potato side of things: frites, gratin dauphinoise, mash, sauté … In fine-dining restaurants, however, I have heard head waiters transform the innocuous and chummy little word 'potato' into a gargle of open contempt that easily can be stretched to five or more syllables pronounced on a descending scale of disgust, the general tone and facial expression suggestive of a deviant and distasteful practice, and one that might easily be punishable in the eyes of the law. The good news is that nearly all restaurants seem at last and finally to have embraced the principle of al dente: the days of pulverized, wet and reeking greens that you could spread on your bread truly do seem to be behind us.

See also: BISTRO, BRASSERIE, FINE DINING, FISH, FRENCH, SERVICE, STEAK

VEGETARIAN AND VEGAN

Cranks. Yes indeed – that was the name of the first vegetarian restaurant in London ever to make any sort of impression. It was way back in 1961, and in Carnaby Street – where else? But Carnaby Street wasn't yet even groovy: the Beatles' first single was more than a year distant, hippies hadn't been thought of, and the peacock male, courtesy of such trendy clothes shops as Lord John, Take Six and John Stephen, was yet to be reinvented. But vegetarianism in those days could not be described as 'cuisine' in any sense of the word at all: what we had here was just all the bits left on the plate after you removed the meat or fish from the picture. Which meant salad. Fruit. Peas. Carrots had a habit of looming large, very often in a lump of cake. Root vegetables, as hitherto crunched up in quantity by pigs. Nuts … a few beans … what we hadn't yet been educated into calling 'pulses' … but hardly enough to keep body and soul together,

Committed vegetarians might want to take warning
from this sixteenth-century painting by Giuseppe Arcimboldo:
take the whole thing too seriously, and it can go to your head.

really. Which I suppose is why to this day you are exceedingly unlikely ever to encounter a fat or even glowing vegetarian: one cannot help thinking it has less to do with health than a kind of enforced self-deprivation of protein. And if my experience of vegetarian and vegan restaurants is anything to go by – and it is so very limited as possibly not to be – you don't see many smiley ones either. Both staff and diners appear to be very intense, though we hope stopping short of eye-rollingly evangelical … You just don't witness a lot of raw and naked love of eating, red in tooth and claw: bloodless, you see – simply not carnal.

Vegan restaurants have to work very hard indeed: no ingredient whatsoever that has any animal connection may be contemplated. So while the more balanced vegetarian will rather tediously admonish you for eating anything with a face, if you so much as presume to put a drop of milk into a vegan's tea, he will have your guts for garters (or, more probably, won't). The eternal puzzle to the carnivore is why such enormous trouble is gone to in order to create usually quite horrible simulations, supposedly in both look and flavour, of the very finest ingredients this planet has to offer: meat, poultry, game, seafood, fish, cheese, eggs, cream, chocolate, on and on and on – all of which must by the vegan be eschewed (as opposed to merely chewed). And, for what you get, such restaurants are always pretty damned expensive.

But vegetarianism is more or less everywhere now, and – like gay marriage – barely remarked upon (except by those who simply never will stop banging on about it). It is impossible to imagine any restaurant that wouldn't offer a reasonable choice of meatless options, so if those are your convictions, you are pretty well catered to, as you know: it's now all a whole lot better than when it was just about Cranks – and even, courtesy of certain image-conscious and apparently newsworthy celebrity ladies, highly fashionable (what with their very public obsessions with such so-called supergrains as quinoa and amaranth, which in such quarters have now wholly taken the place of actual meals). And never you mind that Gordon Ramsay's view is that his 'biggest nightmare would be if the kids ever said: "Dad, I'm a vegetarian." Then I would sit them on the fence and electrocute them.' On a point of etiquette, it is, of course, wrong to try to persuade a veggie to eat a steak (or even a teeny bit of chicken breast, which carnivores seem to think just cannot count), while vegetarians in their turn must always be very, very aware that they must not ever – not once – attempt to noisily foist their tendencies upon the rest of us, nor castigate us for our choices, nor invite us to picture the innocent ickle lamby gambolling in a field. Or even talk about it at all.

See also: ETIQUETTE

WATER

Time was when ordering water in a restaurant marked you down as a cheapskate or a pauper: in those days, water came solely from a tap, and by law it had to be doled out free – whereas even at lunch, wine was the norm. Then came the boom in 'designer water', restaurants very quickly latching on to the immediately uttered offer of 'still' or 'sparkling' (or, as I prefer the choice to be, in order to match one's mood, 'calm' or 'troubled'), this making it deliberately awkward for anyone then to specify 'tap' – i.e. buckshee, as opposed to maybe a fiver. And still: even at lunch, wine was the norm. Then there was the backlash: a vociferous and therefore highly tedious faction started banging on about the stupidity, and then the immorality, and probably even the mortal sinfulness of importing foreign water from thousands of miles away. And so diners who couldn't honestly tell the difference anyway all heaved a collective sigh of relief and happily reverted to ordering 'tap' – thereby demonstrating at a stroke that they were not stupid, but were very moral, and couldn't even dream of committing any sort of sin, mortal or otherwise. And by that time at lunch, wine was no longer the norm: so restaurants' profits suffered a rather severe and immediate double hit.

As ever, what you should order is what you actually like to drink. Do not feel that it is 'wrong' to order Evian if that's what you want (my favourite, actually) – and neither must you feel obliged to order 'tap' because to do anything else might appear a bit flash. Similarly, don't order bottled simply in order not to be thought in any way cheese-paring: just order what you genuinely want. And it must be borne in mind that there is, of course, 'tap' and 'tap': sometimes it's fine, and sometimes it tastes of neglected swimming pool, with just the merest top note of Venice in August. But if it is to be 'tap', then I would love to know why so many restaurants are stubbornly reluctant to leave a jug of the stuff on the table: they give you one glass, and – if you pester them persistently – just might be persuaded to fill it up again.

The brave few are possessed of sufficient chutzpah to order just 'tap' and nothing else whatsoever with a bargain Michelin-starred lunch: there's nothing to say you can't do it ... but ... but ...

See also: **BARGAIN LUNCH, FASHION, WINE LIST**

WEDDINGS

There is the 'intimate' wedding ('No big deal, just family and my very closest friends, all very casual'), at which you will not be eating well, and then there is the 'lavish' wedding ('Oh Christ, we've been planning it all for just *years*! Daddy's going crazy! And everything's going to be just absolutely *perfect*!') ... and you won't be eating well at that one either. Because that's the thing about weddings: they are not about food. Huge thought and planning, respected caterers, and a whole barrel-load of money are involved here, but still they are not about food. The fodder provided shouldn't be actively disgusting, of course – and it helps a great deal if you are a very big fan of champagne and cake – but the focus will always be upon the radiant bride (but of course), as well as, to a far lesser degree, whichever unworthy man it is who has been so very lucky to get her. And then the *placement*, the photographs (the video, God help us), the flowers, the music, the cars ... and of course the ladies' clothes: because many would be more than willing to forego food altogether for the remaining duration of their life on earth in order to be able to buy that sensational wedding outfit, and quite often will be obliged to anyway in order to struggle into it. So: all you really need to do at a wedding is be a polite and smiling guest, eat what is put before you, try not to drink to the degree where you feel you might just be about to fall over, and avoid any act of overt seduction. Do not yawn or roll your eyes during the speeches – and if you are making one, keep it short, and keep it clean. If you happen to be the father of the bride and are actually paying for the whole caboodle, you are free to eat and drink as you desire

– but anyway will be swallowing hard throughout the afternoon, and on into the night.

See also: CELEBRATIONS, FAMILY MEALS, FORMAL DINNERS, ROMANCE

WINE LIST

This can be anything from a very basic footnote on the reverse of a stained and dog-eared menu card, all the way up to an upholstered leather ledger, alive with gold tooling and much tasselation: the weight and bulk of these – nowadays generally seen only in seriously fine res- taurants, or else even more seriously pretentious country-house hotels – would justify a lectern, and were you to devote to them the devout attention they doubtless deserve, you would still be poring over the things long after the chairs are stacked on tables, and the kitchen closed down for the night. You might wonder how any restaurant can hold so amazing a cellar, and the answer is this: either it is a properly fun- ded and regularly replenished wonder that has been there forever and is run by complete and dedicated professionals … or else, a great deal of the finer wines do not actually exist in reality, and are listed just for show. I have encountered this a few times: if, on the off chance, a diner should order a rare and expensive bottle (which perhaps is listed at a relatively modest price), the restaurant will regret that just yesterday they sold the very last one. The truth being that – if they ever stocked it at all – the last bottle was sold simply aeons ago, but its continued pres- ence on the list they imagine contributes a certain grandeur. I know of one long-established and famous restaurant in London that has an arrangement with a nearby wine merchant: should a diner order a posh bottle, some young scullion hares down the road to buy it, shoots back and slips it to the wine waiter – who duly presents it with pride to the punter (pausing only to quadruple the price).

There is but one rule when it comes to the wine list, no mat- ter how humble or grand: order what you want to drink, at a price you are happy to pay (or not too unhappy, at least). House wines, in a decent place, can very often be the best bet (particularly red, and even more particularly Italian) as the restaurant will have tasted a fair few before they lit upon this example, and – because they expect to sell a lot of it – will have negotiated a very good price for bulk, the benefit of which in part (and in theory) they will be passing on to you. Because of the tax and the duty on a bottle, not to say the mark-up, there is no such thing any more as a wine that is actually cheap, but still there is always something that represents good value, within the pressured circumstances. So: do not reject the house because it is the cheapest, and do not fall for that hoary old nonsense about ordering the second cheapest so that the wine waiter and your guest won't immediately mark you down as a skinflint, loser, vagrant and general scumbag. Some cool young places will offer just the four whites and four reds, which will be classified as something along the lines of Good, Better, Great, The Best. Well what's a chap to do? Be guided by the nationality: 'Better' seems for some reason often to be Italian, and generally an improvement on 'The Best', which will usually simply be higher in alcohol content. But do know generally that the higher the price you pay, the more of your money will be going towards the actual wine inside the bottle, and proportionately less to the restaurant and HM Revenue & Customs. No £20 bottle will ever cost much more than £6 in a shop – though you could easily pay £50 in a restaurant for something really good for which a wine merchant would charge maybe £30, or even a bit more. So you see what I mean. As a general rule, if you know nothing about wine, say very little; should your knowledge be extensive, say even less.

Many places now are selling rather interesting and unusual wines by the glass or 50 ml *pichet*, which allows you to dot about a bit. And in quite a few modern restaurants of the more coolly casual variety, the menu will be secondary to the wine list: these are the places to go to if you are keen to experiment, because they take the buying and storage seriously, and there will always be a wide and affordable range, served by and (if you want it) advised upon by eager and knowledgeable people. Sommeliers, of course, are something else entirely, and that's why they merit an entry all of their own, which you might want to glance at …

See also: BYO, SERVICE, SOMMELIERS, VALUE, YOUNG PLACES

WORLD'S 50 BEST RESTAURANTS

Were you hoping to find here an actual list of the world's fifty best restaurants, I am afraid you are in for a disappointment: I would not and could not do such a thing … though others are mightily convinced that they can and must, and so therefore every year we are given The List – which customarily and inevitably is met with a raspberry from anyone who knows anything about restaurants (with the exception, as ever, of those blessed restaurateurs who are chosen). But who decides such things? And – more to the point – which of us has actually visited the fifty in order to make an educated comparison? We can talk only of what we know – and in the 2013 list of fifty, just three are in Great Britain. Three. In a country that is bursting with the greatest chefs and restaurants in its history, as now is internationally recognized. The number one will always be quirky, if not outright weird – somewhere that offers a hundred gimmicky courses to anyone who cares to add his name to the three-year waiting list for a table and is willing to sell his house in order to settle the bill. It's a silly list. Every single year people say it's a silly list. And every single year it unfailingly garners acres of publicity because all the restaurant foodies feel compelled to charge into print in order to reiterate that this list, right …? It's silly.

See also: FORAGING, RESTAURANT CRITICS, RESTAURANT GUIDES, STAR CHEFS, UNUSUAL

X-FACTOR

The X-factor, of course, will vary between each one of us – why, indeed, we call it X: for mystery, for indefinability, an unknown quantity, that thing that you not just know when you see it, but also are hungrily yearning for before even it exists. A lust for a certain type of food that hits you fair and square – straight to the bread basket, which is just the right place. And it will vary not just from person to person but also from occasion to occasion, season to season, morning to night. Because we all know that moment when we are thinking, Mmm … right now, right this very second, I could really murder a … And while it needn't be a curry, we'll certainly know what it is – because at times such as these, all of a sudden, whatever our particular yen, absolutely nothing else will do. Pregnant women get this all the time, apparently (which must actually be a bit of a pain, along with all the others). The X-factor, then, goes way beyond mere hunger: we are talking specifics. Which perhaps in part explains the new popularity of places that specialize: restaurants that sell nothing but rotisserie chicken, say, or steak, with a secret sauce. Or fish and chips. Oh yum – to all of them, each one simmering in the wings, all ready to press our buttons when the lusty occasion arises. So: while X may be said to mark the spot, the X-factor crashes right in to hit that spot – the Greedy Spot, if you like, which lies deep within us all. And which we could, of course, reduce to simply 'G Spot' … except that that has been taken.

YOUNG PLACES

It is a comparatively recent phenomenon: young people now have become the very core, the very mainstay of eating out. They are the future of eating out, and eating out is the only past they know: they were born eating out, they grew up eating out – eating out is what they do. It might be just grabbing a wrap on the street … a burger at the pub … a muffin in a cafe … or they can do the job quite seriously with a gang of like-minded friends in a no-booking fashionable new and rad place, having happily queued to get in there. But it will be a rare day indeed when in some manner or other a young person will not eat out. And so of course it is perfectly natural that an entire new class of restaurants – or eating places, shall we call them, because they don't have much truck with talk of restaurants, the kids – has sprung up to cater to and milk them solely. And these will often dispense utterly with not just comfort, but also, very often, cutlery. Because the worst word of all is 'formal'. Pressed trousers, polished shoes, and a nice smart shirt and tie …? I don't really think so – do you? Softly waved hair in a pageboy, a sensible costume and matching handbag, court shoes and gloves …? Well whaddya think? And so consequently, such as carpets, drapes, soft lighting, tablecloths, candles, napkins, upholstery …? Kidding: you're just going to get jokes about the royal family. Or Liberace. Or worse: you.

What young people like is a bit of rough – in area, as well as wall covering. Driftwood and corrugated iron – they're good. A thudding backbeat that encourages the sauce bottles to do a little jig across the table – that's even better. Hard rock, to echo the rigidity of the benches and stools. Food that's easy to eat. Food that's cool. Food that's hot. In a happening place. But more important than happening – it has to be exclusive, but rather more subtly than actually saying so: simply deliberately disagreeable to anyone who isn't just like themselves. And that means you. Lately, even four walls and a roof is seen to be far too stuffy: the street, that's where they like to be. Hanging. Chilling. Getting down. Eating. Laughing. Texting. Drinking. Tweeting. Smoking. Freezing.

If you yourself are not a young person, you simply won't understand: and you're really not meant to.

See also: BOOKING, CAFES, COMFORT, DECOR, FASHION, GASTROPUBS, OUTDOOR EATING, QUEUING, SMOKING

Young places were different in the 1950s –
and particularly in the United States, where young people were
actually invented, of course. In Britain, we could but gaze upon
such scenes as this in awe, envy and sheer disbelief. I mean,
the table has its very own jukebox, for goodness' sake!

Look: unless you're compiling an A–Z of animals (zebra) or maybe classic movies (*Zulu*), the Z entry is always going to be just a bit of a stretch, so do please be gentle with me. We'd be fine if I was doing food (zabaglione and, um ... well: zabaglione, anyway), but as it's all about eating out, I justify this little gobbet of lyric from *Wannabe*, the debut single from the deathless Spice Girls, thus: after all the cut and thrust of a restaurant meal (the zig-a-zig), there then should steal over you that very rewarding afterglow of repletion (... *ah!*). Like a Bisto Kid. See? You may feel that you've just travelled a zillion miles on a Zimmer frame in order to get to some or other zingy restaurant for a meal you hope will prove to be the zenith of dining experiences. And although the music is unfortunate (the soundtrack to *Zorba the Greek* played on a zither), the place is as busy as a zoo – so you zoom across to that corner table, and good food is zealously served to you. The evening is proving to be zestful, and could just be about to get a little bit zany because you are becoming steadily zonked on a succession of bottles of Zinfandel. There, then, is all of the zig-a-zig. Eventually you leave, a bit muzzy but just this side of dizzy, and zigzag all the way home – where you pop a Zantac, your mind blanks out to zero, and so to bed: zzzzz ... And that's when you should get the ... *ah!*

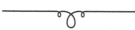

Joseph Connolly is a writer, journalist, book collector
and determined champion of eating out. He is the best-selling author
of twelve novels, including *Summer Things*, *England's Lane* and, the most recent,
Boys and Girls, as well as twelve works of non-fiction, including biographies of
P. G. Wodehouse and Jerome K. Jerome, and a pioneering guide to modern
first editions. For many years he was the proprietor of the Flask Bookshop
in Hampstead, north London, and currently writes a weekly
restaurant review for the *Hampstead & Highgate Express*.